D1610961

ART AND DESIGN IN TEXTILES

ART AND DESIGN IN TEXTILES

MICHAEL WARD

Van Nostrand Reinhold Company
New York · Cincinnati · Toronto · London · Melbourne

TO MY TEACHERS AND FOR JEAN, AARON, ADRIAN AND ALEXANDER

Acknowledgements and thanks to all those who helped me:—

Various Schools at Leicester Polytechnic for
accessibility to knowledge and manufacture of
computer drawings, constructions, textiles,
photographs
The Cosmic Crayon Co. Ltd., Bedford
Alan Gayfer for cycling hours lost and his encouragement
on writing
Sidney Harry for his untiring search to understand colour.
N.A.S.A.
Mr. & Mrs. F. L. Robinson

All diagrams and photographs (and often the contents)
are the work of the author, with the exception of those
acknowledged in the captions. The concern which these
contributors had for the use of their work was a
pleasant revelation which I would like to convey to
the reader

Van Nostrand Reinhold Company Regional Offices:
New York   Cincinnati   Chicago   Millbrae   Dallas
Van Nostrand Reinhold Company International Offices:
London   Toronto   Melbourne

Copyright Michael Ward 1973

Library of Congress Catalog Card Number: 77 39891
ISBN 0 442 29956 7

Designed by Rod Josey

This book is printed in Great Britain by Jolly and Barber
Ltd., Rugby and bound by Webb Son and Co. Ltd.,
Ferndale, South Wales

Published by Van Nostrand Reinhold Company Inc.
450 West 33rd Street, New York, N.Y. 10001 and Van Nostrand
Reinhold Company Ltd., 25–28 Buckingham Gate, London S.W.1E 6LQ

Published simultaneously in Canada by Van Nostrand Reinhold
Company Ltd.

16   15   14   13   12   11   10   9   8   7   6   5   4   3   2   1

CONTENTS

INTRODUCTION

THIS IS NOT A BOOK about the art of textiles. Nor is it a book about the technology of textiles. The reason for writing it is that there is still (and perhaps always will be) a need to bridge the gap between art and technology. Each continues to see the other as its servant, and in extreme cases each may see itself as self–sufficient. I hope this book will help to change this blinkered attitude, though I sometimes think that a spider could make a rope bridge across the Grand Canyon long before teaching could create any significant link between the twin purposes of art and industry. However perhaps these words will reach more students than the few any teacher can have each year.

The principles outlined in the text and illustrations probably apply to other industries as well, but my subject is textiles. More particularly, it is structural textiles. Textile designers reading this will say it has been written by someone brought up in weaving; and they will be right. I spent the first ten years of my working life in Courtauld's historic home in Halstead, Essex, where the fleeing Huguenots from the European lowlands first began weaving in Great Britain.

There the romantic references stop. The joys of handling yarns and fabric cannot be conveyed in words. The romantic cult of hand/art/ weaving is amply dealt with elsewhere. I am writing about facets of interest to everyone using or about to use textiles.

I want to adjust the popular idea of textiles. Brought up against the ideas of new students every September, I am repeatedly aware of the emphases made by their environment and their previous education. There are also many designers who are lost to the textile profession even before they are attracted to an alternative career. Perhaps this is also what the Textile Institute had in mind when in 1970 they created a new qualification which included the word 'design'. As a teacher on the new course, I have the task of presenting students with both sides of the fabric, or network, of knowledge that links art with technology.

As an artist I feel that the climate for such a link is now right, since the sixties finally freed the artist from any particular medium. Even the man in the street is beginning to realize that some very serious artists have rolled up their canvases and have perhaps switched on neon tubes. Some artists feel that their ideas only work well when they rid themselves of human flaws, and the machine with its extra weight or mechanical flawless reproduction can effect this. Moreover, this could result in art for everyman at everyday prices.

However neither the current popular impression of textiles nor any trend away from élitism to art-for-all is absolute, and I hope this book will serve towards making this very foreword out-of-date in a few years. For the rest, I hope that design is timeless, that it means both using existing machinery to the best advantage and producing an idea so good that a machine will be invented to fulfil it.

Design is sometimes working with a specific end use in mind; sometimes an exploitation of, or obsession with, a material. It is thus a problem for the engineer or mechanical man, the inventor or the artist.

This book breaks down into some detail many of the variables which could be dealt with in training and later used intuitively. Alternatively, the variables can be considered and applied consciously to specific problems. At least I hope to show that designing is not just a facile skill of drawing curves and painting pretty colours.

Chapter 1
THE POSITIONS OF
ART AND TECHNOLOGY

EARLY IN THE TWENTIETH CENTURY the civilized web of ideals that art had woven through the centuries was suddenly challenged. The Futurists, downright worshippers of the machine, decided that man's real world was expressed in coal, oil and electricity, the automobile, gun and tank, so they carried on with traditional materials, leaving the Dadaists to spawn an art which destroyed aesthetics and craft.

Take away the craft from a painting and the art should be left – as an idea. Dada found objects and called them art. Duchamp's shock tactics of putting a urinal on show challenged our standards of beauty, and at the same time its position in an art gallery gave us surrealism, the juxtaposition of unconnected objects. The 'isms' in art, like threads, separate, and every now and then one becomes fashionable. Art, through its exhibitions and glossies, is often years ahead of public comprehension and there is only an occasional or superficial feed-off in the applied arts. In the mid-sixties, the black and white theme in textiles, which recurs every few years, overtook Bridget Riley (Fig. 1). Miss Riley survived hefty plagiarism, exploring still the mysteries of the eye, the brain and the heart, but the public gained undigested 'op' prints.

Current textile teaching in art colleges struggles to gain the respect of industry. International art trends in the sixties took on a smoother look. As the creation of ideas dominated and often became separate from the manufacture of the work, so specialist craftsmen were called in. Simultaneously the applied arts were changing from a hand-made, one-off level to design for mass production by employing more teachers with industrial experience. Indeed this thinking started with the Bauhaus as far back as 1919.

The technical college of today offers more than the historic British 'night-school' education to students from industry. A variety of short and long courses are available to students. Because their emphasis is on specialist machinery and technological research, this branch of education is looked to for advice by an industry which is often under-capitalized and which, once it is committed to manufacture, has little time to organize research. On the other side, there is the view of industry. This varies from those employers with enough work to need a designer to those who seem hardly aware that designing is a specialist job and whose large profits prove that they do not need one.

Art-school trained designers do seem to have a history of liability, and their practical work is frequently uneconomic. Their work is not bad, but it is too often difficult to realize satisfactorily on a production

9

Fig. 1 *Fragments, iii.*
Bridget Riley, Tate
Gallery London.

line. The theories that they have been taught do not seem to take into account that 'our firm works this way . . . they come in too late in the morning to help sort out the post . . . they delay the rep. on his daily business . . . they seem to forget we are here to make money, not educate the public'.

Now who is this public whom we all should serve? In the west the public is on the whole more affluent than ever, and through the media it is being decultured regionally and reinfused with a more universal lore. This lore in turn serves to change the wants of the public.

So on one side we have an ivory-towered artist so avant-garde that he can only produce works for other artists, and on the other side Mrs Average, in her thirties, pausing midway between the drapery and the fashion department. All the influence of her past education and the recent pressures of television, press and neighbours are bearing down on her. If the children are patient, not only may she have time to consider whether to have new drapes or a new dress, but also whether she could find an even better bargain somewhere else. Between them is the bewildered industrialist, trying to sell to her.

If she manages to shop around and has a choice, what then will be the deciding factor – good design, the name, the price? Imagine how many people have been involved in the production and promotion of her eventual purchase.

Let us now look at how we arrived here and see if, in doing our job, our priorities are right. To do this, imagine how such a situation may have begun.

It probably began a bit later than the garden of Eden, when the fig-leaf stage was past. Having found that animal skins (his and hers) kept them warm, this couple, Fred and Elsie, pushed off to live a little further north. Animals abounded and the skins began to pile up as they ate their way through large steaks. One day Elsie found they had neighbours.

'What do you think they've done with all their spare animal skins?' she exclaimed on returning home to Fred. 'They've hung them all round the cave, gee, it's so cosy – they still light the fire at night to keep away the sabre-toothed tigers of course, but they don't need it really what with all those holes blocked with bits of fluff off of the carcases.'

'Half a mo,' grunted Fred, realizing that civilization was beginning to take place and stalling long enough to think of an idea that would match that of the Jones's. 'Half a mo,' he said, dragging by its hair half a mohair goat into the firelight (Fig. 2). Clutching at the hair in the same way that people now clutch at a straw, he cried with an enthusiasm that was but a thin frothy veil that barely hid the stone wall of his desperation, 'But how would you like to have a coat of these smooth, warm hairs?' And having offered the goods for sale, so to speak, he had to provide them to maintain the goodwill.

How he managed we will never know, as he had no Rumpelstiltskin the technician to come to his rescue. But whatever posterity owes to the notorious destroyers who come in the autumn of empires and cut down the established and the rotting to make space for the new and vital, it owes more to the Freds and Elsies, the constructors whose skills survive each revolution.

Returning to Fred and Elsie's cave, here they have found the solution to the improvement of their wellbeing by (1) shaping a skin, 'fashioning' it to use the word in a truer if more archaic sense; (2) constructing, by weaving the hair, a textile piece which was afterwards

Fig 2 'Half a mo'.

fashioned into a garment; (3) insulating their environment (hanging up skins); (4) gaining spiritual satisfaction by making marks on their surfaces which, it is thought, told stories, willed animal capture, recorded numbers and events, and made symbols of praise and thanksgiving. All of these marks had a by-product: decoration.

Their counterparts today are highly complex people working intelligently and thriftily all their lives without a fig (leaf?) for the past unless it be for our habit of turning back a few decades or occasionally a century or two and romanticizing – but more of that later.

The fashion/textile trade uses materials and methods as old as Fred and Elsie's civilization, and their four solutions carry on independently with their own rules and their own broad limits.

1. Fashion. The very word now covers the desire, encouraged by the tempo of life and the money to spend, for change. There are many categories, from the 'haute couture' women able to indulge their whims, through the 'rag trade' to the tramp who is grateful for the warmth of cast-off socks.

How many different garments are there in your wardrobe? There are many more specialized people involved in putting them there. Each operation may be a job which was learned in a few days or a skill which only became commercially practicable after years. It may also be an operation dependent on flair and a developed knowledge of the particular requirements of the market.

2. The same applies to the textile trade, but here the specialities have evolved from both the person to clothe and the environment to fill.

If the initiative is taken by the textile manufacturer, it is within the limits of a problem for which he thinks the maker-up or the interior designer has a solution. Occasionally the set-up is ideal for another outlet. Take the case of the invention of the parachute, for example. This is a life-saver of delicate appearance, the embodiment of many qualities that textiles have, and an example of a use which grew out of existing machinery. The astronaut's glorious return is because of the weight and the precise ratio of yarn and air flow to control the dropping speed of his capsule. (All that way to be let down by a few threads!)

3. Having decided that insulating the cave was a good idea, it doesn't really matter whether you use skin (leather), hair (cloth), or today's expanded polystyrene, because you are approaching the job from 'outside'. You are not limited by given materials or media, by physical machinery, or the machinery of distribution to get it home.

In this century Man has begun to reconstitute natural elements to make many new materials superior in some ways to the originals. But he is strangled by economic or social pressures, or perhaps just by non-thinking.

A modern dining chair need not be a plastic seat with a back and four legs made with the thinking that went into wood. It should be designed to give the body the minimum strain and the alimentary organs their best chance to carry out their digestive duties. (This could, of course, lead to questioning the need for a dining table!) Thus for the chair a new material with its own properties could be used in the best way. For unadventurous manufacturers there is a ready public who take comfort in a world of illusion and want easy-care plastic with the atmosphere of wood. But occasionally someone designs a new object for which the material or method is *chosen*. He is not strait-jacketed by a company who have always used a particular process or material.

This kind of opportunity seems to occur at two ends of the scale: one, where unforeseen needs arise, as when vast corporations make an Apollo moon rocket, or two, where one man with an eye to the main chance says, 'Here is a new material. Can I create a new end use because of its peculiar qualities?' This applies particularly in the toy trade. Or, 'Here is a new material. I can run a line of things in that and sell them cheaper than in the traditional material.' Such a man can do this. He employs new people. He has no obligations other than a reasonable code of professional behaviour, and providing he doesn't tie up too much money in capital or specialized machinery which he may be left with if the project fails, he is set.

In between these two extremes of the corporation and the individual lie all the orthodox established set-ups for processing a particular material and manufacturing a particular object. Using a new material means that an established manufacturer, apart from having to find the space and money for new machinery, has to divert labour and management to cope with the new situation. He may then fall down when he realizes that the new product merely supplants his present product without necessarily increasing his immediate sales and profits. Indeed he may even have to sack old operatives and lose goodwill.

4. Spiritual satisfaction enters into this; I have deliberately used the word 'spiritual', though it is here that many would-be readers and the book might part company. It arouses cynicism from both Joe on his market stall and Jeremy in college. Until this century art was, generally speaking, a job that called for highly developed craft skills. Only recently, has it been able to begin to shake off its association with virtuosity, skills or facility.

No one now really expects two-dimensional illusions of faces or landscapes. Art is no longer a brass monkey, exposed to the cold gaze of the layman critic and his 'what's it supposed to be?', though the larger public still look for this sort of visual translation of familiar objects though they wouldn't dream of doing this with music. Even with pop music the sounds are 'abstract' – they exist for their own sake and make little attempt to describe or imitate bird songs or other recognizable natural sounds. The value of art comes from the quality of its idea, but the manufacturer tries to sell his product using the cheapest labour and the cheapest materials possible. With 'classier' goods perhaps less importance is attached to this, since time, convenience or service are worth more than minute material savings. However, generally speaking, in mass production it is more worthwhile to cut down on extravagant operations or materials. These nibble away a little more profit from each similarly produced item.

The most difficult designing of all therefore – thinking still of the quality of the idea behind the design – is for the simplest and cheapest. This is probably because the manufacturer either cannot or will not find a designer capable of doing the job. Occasionally a '10 cent' item is not badly designed, and even actually pleasing – that is, by my standards. And it is personal standards I want to touch on next.

You must constantly see your own opinion in relation to the opinion of the majority of the chosen market. Designers, like artists, often design well for themselves or each other and then make a hash of designing for other people. Conversely, it is difficult for the student designer to leave the academic warmth of college, where he had time to discuss the implications of his products (and didn't?), to thrash along misunderstood in a workaday world. He may have to try to convince his boss that if a particular stripe came a millimetre lower, 'and that curve was a little less sudden', they would then have a product that both the mass market and the top end of the market could not fail to resist. Such sensitivity to proportions or colour or some other aesthetic quality can be dealt with as a science, and I will contribute one or two formulae for success. Alternatively a designer apprenticed from school who grows up knowing a particular market and designs adequately for it, can find difficulty in a new situation. And what of the student who arrives in college with a high sensitivity or a background of 'good taste'? He may spend miserable years trying to adapt, trying to shake off his cosy habits and increase his awareness of other requirements, and at the end he may still lack the patience or toughness to accept the cruel limitations of industry. So do you see what I mean about the word 'spiritual'? It is, I believe, one way of expressing an education in art. 'Spiritual' should involve the student understanding both the never-changing factors that are important to his subject and the ever-changing emphasis that particular times may bring.

Finally, as near professional equipment and conditions as possible should be used at some stage in college, not just to produce 'professional' looking work but to bring typical problems home in a real way, so that the student is a little more prepared for real work on leaving college. For the spirit of industry is totally different from the caveman's scratchings. They gave him comfort outside the material needs of food and shelter. Understanding why some surface marks, patterns, designs or layouts are more attractive than others may account for some of the effect of the sale of graphics and textile prints. But there are so many sophisticated associations bound up with the success of such operations that it is almost impossible to establish scientifically a formula for their workings. Nevertheless the actual marks made today are largely just decorative, and, however prima donna a student becomes about his designs, it is really often only a case of one person's decoration being chosen in preference to another by one section of the public.

Students in art-college conditions are often encouraged to pursue their individual qualities. I hope this is mainly because it develops their self-confidence, which is as it should be, but it is a hangover from a half-century of high-ego expressive art, and it is also in opposition to the technical/vocational type of course. This last in the short term may give industry a designer trained to work for existing machinery, but in the long term he may have little understanding of the broad picture.

A designer has a constant battle between his own powers of creativity and the medium, machinery and means of distribution, before his ideas are realized. If they ever are!

Chapter 2
THE WHOLE OBJECT

THIS CHAPTER is about the beginning and the end of designing and what it encompasses.

From birth we are conditioned into thinking that objects are 'whole' (Fig. 3). A baby may think her face is the 'whole' of his mother, a spoonful of food is seen as a whole to be sucked clean. The spoon may then take on the appearance of something which is repeated, until the baby is literally 'fed up'. If the baby could reason, he would see the whole meal as complete – as a whole object – in much the same way that in later life he quickly takes in a page, a book or the duration of a television film, or three minutes of a disc on the turntable.

We are always in danger of making judgements on objects which have strong and often quite unnecessary conventions of entity. A painting is usually a rectangle and may be 12 inches × 8 inches or 80 inches × 120 inches. You can talk about its composition, i.e., the relationship of the parts to the whole. If it were a landscape there might be a great deal of talk about the subject matter, realism, mood, colour, texture, style, paintwork etc., but nothing at all about its being a flat rectangle. Yet neither our vision nor our thoughts would naturally take on a recti-linear form, even in an age when almost every gadget or object is box-shaped or packaged. We have so accepted the painting convention that there may be only a handful of artists who have tried to show us that the two-eyed view of the world is something else. It is more likely a very blur-red ellipse with a changing sharp focal point. If you don't believe this, try making a drawing of, say, a light switch on the far side of a room and fill in as much around it as you can. But look only at the switch and your drawing.

Having challenged a basic convention of picture making, let us try it with a dress. You can certainly regard a dress as a whole object, but you don't do it like this. Vaguely you have an idea that the dress is on a female form who is probably wearing shoes. She is? Now take off her shoes. See how the dress appears to change! It belongs to a different person. She may now look silly, sexy, lazy or in the process of dressing or undressing, all according to what you saw in the first place.

So I think you will agree that it is better to design for an 'ensemble' when possible. You think of shoes and stockings. Then when you have considered head gear or hairstyle you can plan the wardrobe. How ingenious are you at buying a garment which you can afford and also use with your existing clothes? Another way of designing is to plan a range. You may buy other people's designs and call yourself a design

Fig. 3 *Still Life with Gingerpot 1 and 2.* Mondrian. From birth we are conditioned into thinking that objects are 'whole'. Mondrian abstracts but has to face the problem of specifying objects.

producer. You then plan a range or collection for your 'house' or company.

Designing for an occasion – a 'whole' event – shows how designing is a curious welding of the material to the abstract. This is made clearer if you can imagine your favourite sport or ceremony with someone taking part wearing appropriate clothing. Now think of that person in the same outfit but in everyday life, and see how awkward he looks.

But textile design alone may not afford such an opportunity. Because our society is so specialized, the textile designer may never be more than a source of raw materials. He may have to use some rectangular motif – a painting – and because the fabric is going to be mass-produced it needs to be 'put in repeat'. Now! If an artist has taken great pains fitting his ideas into a rectangle, is it likely that they will work if there is even the suggestion of a repeat or the hint of a fold in the surface? He becomes the victim of a personality cult which uses famous names in an attempt to associate painting with textile design.

Art and design then, are they separate or fused? This question must arise because both art and technical institutions teach textile design. It is dangerous either to separate art from design or to superimpose one on the other. Serviceable fabrics may be knitted or woven if all the technical requirements are met, e.g., a machine will demand that threads are smooth enough or strong enough, and common sense will help you find a thread that is smooth and strong. By using a mundane and practical, rather than a sensitive and practical, approach, a strong fabric in an attractive colour may be produced. It may be easy to run. It may be a huge commercial success. In a highly competitive market, however, the rare event of this being consistently repeated would indicate that the designer was a complete natural, literally a freak with an uncanny sense of market trends.

Visitors to the textile trade are often alarmed at the string-and-cardboard attitude in some productive areas. On the other hand, they underestimate how much any one business depends on the slowly evolving bread and butter of repeat orders and gentle modifications. A designer might work desperately hard, but only his more spectacular efforts will make news. Art-pure let loose in such a business could do more harm than good; its essential anarchy could destroy both security and goodwill.

Bread and butter lines exist, however, more through efficiency and special know-how than flair. So much so, that a machine working and a worker busy tend to take priority over a product. Oh! of course the fabric will be fault free.

With 99 per cent of energy devoted to efficiency, it is not surprising that having *just* the right shade of 'fashion' blue is overlooked. The designer may beat on the side of the truck taking the rolls of fabric to the store. He may still be unheard at the meeting afterwards, where they try to discover why the housewife has bought a competitor's fabric in preference to their own. Here they will examine the price and delve into costs and production efficiency. Efficiency is concerned with the amount of time the machine is running. It is measured as a percentage of the machine's maximum capacity, and combined with fail-safe stop motions you have fault-free fabric. A string is often put in the edge of a piece of fabric to denote a fault. With many customers only accepting one or two such strings in fifty yards, some idea of usual standards can be seen. Fibre, yarn and fabric strength are all measurable, wet or dry, pulled or rubbed. Delivery dates may be checked to measure service. These are facts: but how can you measure the customer who passes by your goods because your blue is a little too sharp or a little too faded? How do you measure something that doesn't happen?

A much worse state of affairs occurs when you add art to textiles. I don't mean the honest gimmick. That is preferable to lip service or clumsy handling of a subject for which you have little feeling. Dogmatic teaching leads to fables like 'blue and green should never be seen'! Such dynamic ideas on design education as the Bauhaus may have had fifty years ago, have produced perhaps ten generations of teachers teaching teachers, so that it is a wonder that anything worthwhile has survived. Luckily, right things are taught for wrong reasons, and the average student's age, 18 to 22, puts self-understanding high up with academic scholarship. Foreign travel, extra-mural activity, mixed lodgings and even the coffee break all contribute greatly to the student's development.

Textiles can, despite the difficulties, be a medium of art. There is a conflict of purposes in art schools between the extremes of those supporting an industry and those who see textiles as an extension of art – perhaps as an alternative medium to painting. In between the two, there are those who consider that it doesn't matter what students learn so long as they improve themselves. While some artists try to put any skill they have in second place behind a worthwhile idea.

But once you commit yourself to a technique, then you must learn to work within the chosen technique's bounds. Eventually you will probably go all through its groundwork, and with an ancient craft like weaving the prospect of breaking new ground at an early stage is not very high. But the subject appeals to people who want to make something useful and those who see romantic connections, and there are many books of instructions on 'how to do it' with knitting and weaving. I would prefer to ask what do textiles offer?

Consider the traditional fine art media and how they help us see our world.

Etching invites fine lines, directness of approach, chemical control or virtuosity with the hand (Fig. 4). Printing with screens, line or wood,

Fig. 4 Etching invites fine lines.

18

Fig. 5 *Macrogauze 63.*
Peter Collingwood.

offers flat massive areas, registration, repetition, transparency and opacity. Painting allows for a larger size, a better chance to modulate and change areas as you go along. Weaving *can* give fine lines when the threads are both fine and dense. Pictures, as in Stevengraphs, may be woven and repeated perfectly but massive areas are more applicable. Free arrangements of colours are difficult, unless they fall in stripes or the colours are analogous. It can give optical colour, can be highly textured and is drapable.

The twentieth-century West has given 'Art' to all. The fact that anyone can practise art is even more significant. The employed medieval craftsman has been left behind, and the artist of today, although perhaps financially leaning on teaching or some other work, needs no patron.

Many an artist may have been 'hooked' on etching by the smell of acid, on pottery by the softness of clay. It is a pity that there has been little apparent contribution to twentieth-century art through the medium of textiles. Most of the 'names' have achieved little which they could not have done with paint, though the soft sculpture of Claes Oldenburg and the hangings by Peter Collingwood (Fig. 5) are notable exceptions. Though totally different, their respective works have techniques, material and subject matter that are interdependent. Many other devotees to textiles have been lesser artists using secondhand subject matter. The texture peculiar to fabrics has often been incidental in the interpretation of painting forms. The current preoccupation with 'idea' rather than techniques means that textile design may not attract the best artists because the technique is slow and demanding – and limiting. But three developments could create new interest: the gradual increase in leisure time, the reaction against mass-produced and synthetic goods, and the production of cheap home knitting machines.

What you are going to do with an object decides what it should look like – unless you are being deliberately perverse and, say, want to design a cushion that looks like a dog. This may be cute or thought of as bad taste. It may be much nearer to art in the sense that it does not conform to the rules of functional design. But pretending a manufactured object is something else is unimportant to true design, unless your starting point is that sort of market – not a bad point for a student to consider when he begins to run out of idealism.

The true starting point of design, however, is found not in what an object is called, but in what it does. A cup can be almost any hollow shape, but its function is to contain liquid (perhaps boiling) temporarily before transmitting it to the mouth. Afterwards it is cleaned or thrown away. What it does is its design. What it looks like is its style.

An artist sets his own problems with or without chosen material or machinery in mind. He may proceed with empathy, that is, by feeling his way, which often looks as if he doesn't know what he is doing. The act of creativity is indeed seldom truly conscious and therefore may be hard to measure. Thomas Edison had great empiricism and a show of lateral thinking that would delight an artist. He had an immense junk pile for his experiments and a team to search the world for grass fibres and monkeys' hairs – he knew he wanted a filament for his incandescent light. Edison was designing.

Revelations, like the apple that fell on Sir Isaac Newton's head and caused the discovery of the force of gravity, only come after years of patient work. In hind sight this looks painfully slow. Look at the dates on the Mondrian paintings (Figs. 6–12). He followed the styles of his age and at thirty-six painted the first one illustrated here. It took four more years before his significant year, 1912, during which he lost the 'thing' in his painting – in this case the tree. But see how it took another nine years to produce a Mondrian as perhaps you think of him – the beautiful *non*-geometric adjustments to achieve equilibrium. In the score of years that followed, he consolidated his work, all the time 'thinking with his eyes'.

But let us go back to the painting fallacy. Accepting the fact that 'art' is more than representations on canvas, it does, however, give us, in the majority of cases, objects whose size is bound fairly closely to the human being. If it is intimate or delicate, it will be 3 feet × 2 feet and fill our world at a distance of 3 feet. But it may be as big as a man can stretch to or throw his paint on.

The first communication of a design for a textile may well be

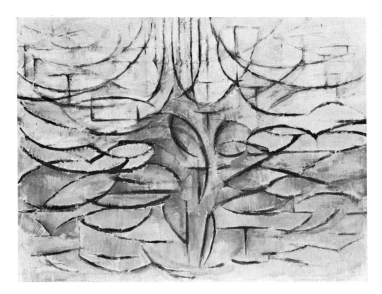

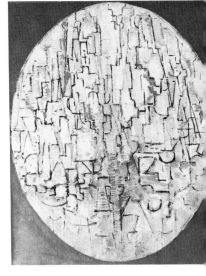

Fig. 8 **1912**. *Flowering Appletree*. Mondrian, Gemeentemuseum The Hague.

Fig. 9 **1913**. *Oval Tree Composition*. Mondrian, Stedelijk Museum Amsterdam.

expressed in paint on a sheet of paper, trimmed into a rectangle, mounted neatly on card, put in a case with ninety-nine more and hawked round the manufacturers. A tie manufacturer has to imagine the chalky paint glistening like dyed silk, the effect of a knot and its width and the tie cut diagonally across this shape. He must, of course, see the tie as a component in the 'whole' outfit of a man.

Dress textiles are nearly always cut up to fit the human body in a special way. Usually there is some form of draping, as in curtaining. Forms that are either beautiful or insignificant when a textile is stretched flat for printing or under tension on a loom, take on a new life when in proper use (Fig. 13). But there is a terrible temptation in the world of the textile designer to prejudge designs at an early stage.

Fig. 6 **1908**. *The Red Tree*. Mondrian, Gemeentemuseum The Hague.

Fig. 7 **1912**. *The Grey Tree*. Mondrian, Gemeentemuseum The Hague.

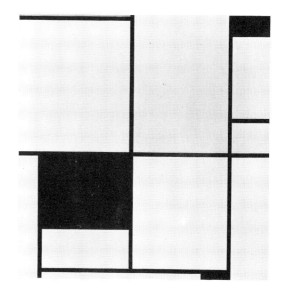

Fig. 10 **1913/14**. *Composition in Oval*. Mondrian, Gemeentemuseum The Hague.

Above right: Fig. 11 **1921**. *Composition I with red, yellow and blue.* Mondrian, Gemeentemuseum The Hague.

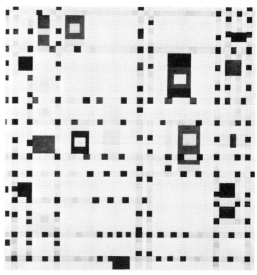

Fig. 12 **1942/43**. *Broadway Boogie Woogie*. Mondrian, The Museum of Modern Art, New York.

Art is usually about ideas of phenomena, illusion, the literal, the active, the symbolic. . . . The content of a painting is usually so strong that it is difficult to remember afterwards whether it was on board or canvas. Except for specially placed motifs or emblems, textiles are usually chopped about to make a nonsense of picture-making. Anyway what could be a more devastatingly powerful 'canvas' than a beautiful woman. She becomes sculpture and moves. Your 'picture' takes on her form or drapes, and it is different when you move. It moves when *she* moves. Rather complicated for the little painted sketch that we started with!

So much of the high price paid for art is for the rarity value, which puts art on a high pedestal. The similarity here with Paris gowns is obvious, particularly where it is the first (publicized) artist who takes the credit for leading art. His disciples follow and consolidate his concepts with their ideas. In a similar way, the stores copy haute couture. In both cases modifications are made, and often ingenuity and originality shine through, but the *big move* has already been made, the theme has been played.

One of the biggest fallacies that needs correcting is that textile designing is putting a motif into repeat. Starting with a picture or motif is totally wrong, especially for a beginner. Understandably, this idea grows out of picture making and needs to be corrected in nearly every student. A 'motif' seen once or perhaps nearly twice on a garment will pass the eye, but usually it is seen many times, when the eye picks up a *rhythmic flow* of lines or spots but not the beautiful motif! When these lines or spots are non-significant details, we call them 'unwanted repeat marks', and the good professional designer eliminates or avoids these. But 'picture' making or 'whole' concept conditioning is so strong, that it takes students months to adapt to repeating designs and even longer to have reasonable control over their marks.

It may have been forced on me by the process, but I now get endless fascination from using elements of design which start with rhythm and are often then only thinly disguised. There is a security in the unsophisticated rhythmic beat (Fig. 14). We succumb to this sensation with a genteel waltz, reggae, rock, or a healthy cycle ride.

But it is also easy to carry repetition and order too far, so that you

Fig. 13 Forms take on a new life when in use.

Fig. 14 There is a security in the unsophisticated rhythmic beat.

are putting things into smaller repeats than is necessary. There is no technical reason why every thread in a width of weaving should not be a different colour. There is often no reason why garments should not be asymmetric – with different legs like a harlequin. While embroidery departments in colleges continue to outweigh their industrial counterparts, there is a chance that new design ideas will germinate. At their worst they produce more hackneyed results than any other. At their best, such departments can keep alive mental processes which are less likely to be overwhelmed by machinery limitations.

Numbers affect design. It is worth spending time paring away extravagancies in a prototype. Theoretically the longer the intended run, the more the manufacturer can afford to spend on any design. This could mean that it is just right for Mr Average, yet not *quite* right for everyone else. Mass production means flawless finishes are obtainable as each process is more and more refined. Artists reacting against the 'prima donna' image by seeking an anonymous look, have hence turned to plastic finishes instead of brush-marks. There is therefore a sort of chicken and egg relationship between mass production and art-for-all.

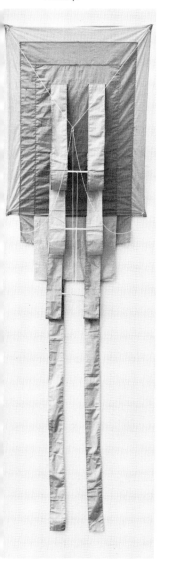

Fig. 15 *Multiple*. Kite designed by Robyn Denny to mark the 75th anniversary of the Tate Gallery.

We have seen a great increase in print-making – the traditional media of etching, screen and lithography. But a new form has arrived – limited (or unlimited) editions of '*multiples*', i.e., repeated three-dimensional objects often made by moulding techniques (Fig. 15). Textiles in fashion form have expanded their middle area to parallel this. The traditional élitists of Paris, with attendant large mass-producers, have lost publicity to areas where the big money changes hands, in the boutiques of Carnaby Street one year, Kings Road the next, wherever youth goes.

I have been dealing with aspects of conditioning of thought in art and textiles, with repetition and entity. Emphases change, machines may alter, people can alter in their needs, but what is common ground? What can never be taken away?

The answer is abstract elements such as colour, tone, line, mass, proportion and texture. They are aesthetic qualities for which rules could be made, providing they are broken every day in the interests of a richer life. Artists will tend to part company here, because their life-long job is *not* to define, even if they then immediately break the rules. The fear, too, of being thought 'decorative' is transmitted yearly to hundreds of students going into the – for want of a more apt description – decorative arts. Even when fashion has mocked all the traditional ideas of good taste, there must still be 'constants' left to be learned.

Well, perhaps it isn't learning so much as investigating, with a three-part process. The first is being made aware of the qualities common to art and textiles, and *caring* about them. The second is making individual and personal comments about these qualities and using them, sometimes in the abstract, sometimes in conjunction with specific limitations such as machinery. The third is having enough control to be able to use them to suit *other* people's requirements while retaining one's own individuality and integrity. It is rather like taking a child to a football match, showing him that there's fun to be had kicking a ball around, and pointing out the niceties. You let him have a kick too, and then show him the rules. When he's a man making money at it, playing for the manager, to the crowd, he should still be having fun.

23

Chapter 3
BIT BY BIT

DESIGNING TEXTILES is essentially constructing a large unit from many small elements. Designers tend to prefer to work with immediately visually rewarding effects. Painting-trained designers will try to 'rough-out' and gradually 'fine-down' their work. Building from components is different. It often calls for patient work – like bricklaying with a new type of brick, the effect of which won't be seen till the wall is up. The textile process may be one where the designer does not have full control over the machinery. You will see that any minute modification or mistake applied to one component will be multiplied many times over and become really noticeable – not necessarily as a mistake, but as an overall change of character. Building is, therefore, at least as valuable a

Below left: Fig. 16 Unit building: part of a Roman floor at Chedworth, Gloucestershire.

Below: Fig. 17 Unit building to make a tapestry weave and a man with a beard.

Fig. 18 Unit building:
an Irish wall.

Fig. 19 Unit building:
iron and glass.

Fig. 20 Unit building:
wood store.

starting principle as simply interpreting a painting or painterly qualities into a print, or the bark of a tree into weaving (Figs. 16–20).

I shall mainly show how the appearance is affected by the physical make-up (Fig. 21). You are likely to associate certain fibres with special jobs: nylon for tights, flax for canvas. Nylon, though, could be the bristle in a toothbrush or a bearing for a wheel, and flax could make a delicate translucent lawn dress. Just consider the sand from the pit that was transformed into your clear, brittle window. The same grab-load may have made the marbles that were eventually turned into those swaying folds of glass fibre that decorate the window edges. They are both the same material! Why are they different? Think of a bicycle-chain made of stiff half-inch links. If you take an end in each hand it droops – easily. The links are upright and the bearings are free. Now straighten the chain, twist it a quarter turn and it still droops – though not so much. It is not meant to be so flexible in this direction. What is important is the way one element is connected to its neighbour (Fig. 22).

Above: Fig. 21 Physical make-up: sackcloth or a very expensive wool and silk mixture?

Fig. 22 What is important is the way one element is connected to another: a suspended bicycle chain.

The visual effect of textiles is dependent on the physical, which is the inherent nature of the raw material plus the linkage. A net curtain or a blanket may be made from the same fine nylon fibres. Academically it should be possible to weave sackcloth out of wool, cotton, polyester, polyamide, rayon, or even silk, by juggling around with the construction of the different component yarns.

But to begin at the beginning, I will now follow the path from molecule to fibre, to yarn, to fabric. As I aim to show that there are

26

Fig. 23 Spinning by parallelizing and twisting staple fibres.

Fig. 24 Spinning by extruding a viscous solution through a spinneret.

Fig. 25 An average textile molecule can be thought of as a bicycle chain.

many *variables* which can influence the design and subsequent appearance of a fabric, I shall be writing a continuous glossary of terms. Their first appearance will be shown in capitals, and a definition will be given. Counting these terms will be a quick way of counting the number of bricks on the path to a textile. You can then skip this chapter unless you are intrigued by the bewildering world that the designer could, but doesn't have to, live in – well, not all of it anyway.

To start, there is MOLECULE: simply a minute group of atoms (which I won't attempt to define). STAPLE FIBRE: a short length of single thickness textile material, $\frac{1}{2}$ inch – 20 inches long. FILAMENT: (virtually) continuous fibre. YARN: a collection of staple fibres or filaments ready for use to make a fabric. FABRIC here refers to MATERIAL, though material, like MACHINERY, may sometimes be used in the abstract sense. Let's now clear up one difficult etymological point: the word SPIN. According to the context this can mean two things. One is twisting fibres together, necessary to make a yarn from staple (Fig. 23), the other is passing a viscous fluid through holes in a spinneret (a finely perforated nozzle) and drying the resultant filaments (Fig. 24).

The smallest effective part of a textile is the long chain molecule. This could be about 0.005 mm long and 0.000007 mm in width. As this means nothing to me either, I'll be happier telling you that there would be 400 end to end across the middle of a pin head and 2,800,000 side by side. This happens quite naturally in the cellulosic fibres such as the seed hair from cotton. An average textile molecule can now be thought of as a bicycle chain laid over an Olympic discus throw with each link as a group or ring of atoms (Fig. 25). The molecule can be straight or crimped. If it is crimped, it can be more or less straightened by stretching.

This happens, for example, in wool and nylon. When you stop stretching a wool molecule, it returns to its former state. With nylon, it depends when you do it.

Nylon for bearings differs from textile nylon in that the molecule chains are at random. There is no 'grain'. When a man-made yarn is made, it is from a viscous fluid which is pumped through the minute holes of a spinneret. The instant it leaves the holes, the chains begin to parallelize. The process of drawing off filaments conveniently makes grain and improves its textile qualities. The length of the molecule is increased up to about ten times, dragging the chains more and more parallel. Forces of attraction become stronger as the chains get closer and closer.

Parallelization is also a contributing factor in making brightness, as will be shown in Chapter 7. Whereas natural fibres are difficult to modify, you can see that in man-mades even the same raw material can be adjusted to produce a new yarn. RAYON (made from regenerated wood or cotton cellulose) was an early yarn which, when stretched in the making, made a stronger, less stretchy yarn suitable for auto-tyres. An even greater complication is to graft on branches or side chains with other chemicals. As the stem is pulled the branches lag. The stem returns

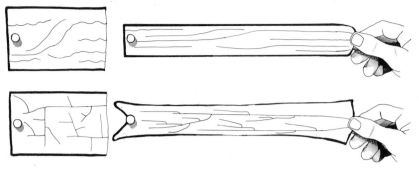

Top: Fig. 26 Stretching the fibres which parallelize molecule chains, increasing strength as the molecules close up and attract each other.
Bottom: in fibres where the molecules have side chains the new form is not taken up, and when tension is released they behave like elastic.

when the tension is taken off. The first ELASTIC fibres were made in this way (Fig. 26).

Luckily for colour lovers the molecule chains are seldom perfectly parallel or even close. Areas with large holes, AMORPHOUS regions where the molecules are disordered, allow first the water and then the dye molecules in. Much of the fibre character depends on the subtleties of the areas which may change imperceptibly from dyeable amorphous to non-dyeable CRYSTALLINE.

In man-made yarns colour can be added to the mix before it is pushed through the spinneret. This internal or SPIN DYEING (or dulling by a white pigment) is permanent and even. In traditional dyeing the problems involve the variables of amounts and sizes of amorphous spaces. Also, dye molecules vary in size. Wetting and heating modifies the fibre molecules, allowing the dye to get in (and out again) (Fig. 27). Fibre or filament shape will greatly affect the final appearance (see Chapter 7).

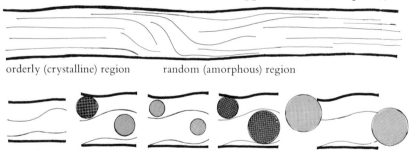

orderly (crystalline) region   random (amorphous) region

amorphous regions with dyestuff – dark ones successful

Fig. 27 Some molecules can't get in, some get in and stay, some go in and out again straight-away.

Most man-mades are manufactured with specific purposes in mind. An acrylic designed for dresses will need more dye for a deep shade than a carpet would need. The reason is that for a given size of thread the number of filaments may differ. The many fine filaments on a dress fabric yarn add up to a larger surface area to bounce back the light and make the yarn appear pale. The few coarse filaments of a carpet show a richer colour (Fig. 28).

From the previous statement comes another vital and easily understood aesthetic quality – drape. If you compare electricians' house wire with cleaner flex, you will find that the first is stiff – it only needs to bend once when it is fitted – and the second, as the name implies, is flexible. Take off their overcoats and you will see that the house wire is made of three components which have a meagre number of filaments, while in the cleaner cable the many filaments are allowed to slide independently of each other. Clearly a stiff yarn will not bend or drape like a flexible one.

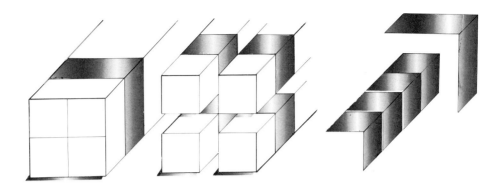

Fig. 28 A given weight (size) of yarn may be made with few filaments (square section on left) or many filaments (four-square section, middle). The surface area, which may be regarded as mirrors, of the four-square section is much greater than that of the square section, as will be seen by the isolated 'mirrors' on the right.

But before we get involved with yarn, there are a few more physical variables that could be mentioned. There are various tests made to measure the qualities of fibre, yarn and fabric. Many of these measurable variables affect the function and the tactile rather than the visual qualities.

TENACITY is a measurement of strength relative to weight (density). Stop and think about this. It is usually applied to fine tests on fibre or yarn.

TENSILE STRENGTH is a measurement of strength relative to area. You can talk of lb per sq. in. breaking strain.

EXTENSION or 'elongation at break' is how much a yarn 'gives' or increases in length at breaking point. There are two possible figures: one when the yarn is being made (the plastic state), and one when in use. If it is stretched at the making stage, it will become stronger, but it is less likely that you would be able to stretch it in use. Polyamide/polyester ropes for rock climbers or auto seat-belts must 'give' just enough to cushion shock. But once they have been used as life savers, they should be discarded because of the discomfort or worse that may occur on the next occasion.

ELASTICITY is the ability of a fibre to recover from strain. Rubber has awkward shaped molecules which must return after stretching out of the normal shape. All fibres have measurable extension and elasticity.

Although technology need have no aesthetic opinion (it may have no love for touch or appearance), it can predict from the appearance of a STRESS–STRAIN CURVE just how a fibre will feel and look when used (Fig. 29). A curve of a stress–strain diagram shows that fibres do not

Fig. 29 Each type of fibre has its own stress/strain curve. How it 'gives' and how much weight is required to effect this accounts for the subtleties of draping as well as its strength.

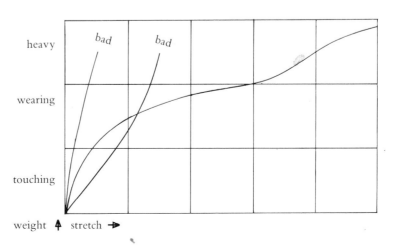

29

extend evenly as more and more weight is applied. If they did, then the 'curve' would be a straight line. Some fibres 'give' easily, under the merest touch they will seem soft. A slightly heavier load involves COMPLIANCY, the measurement of the reduction of stiffness over a moderate stretch or bend. If this is high then the fibre falls easily into the new position, it feels good and drapes well.

HANDLE of animal-hair fibres is affected by their one-way-only effect of growing, known to technologists as 'directional frictional effect' (*D.F.E.*). (Fig. 30).

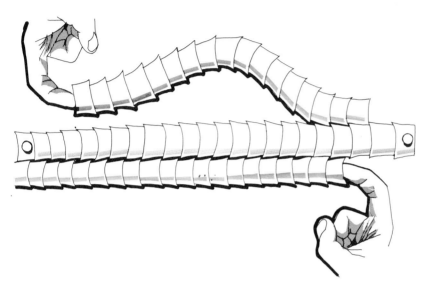

Fig. 30 D.F.E. or directional frictional effect. Both the handle and the movement of animal fibres is affected by the one-way-only touch. Felting is effected when the fibres are rubbed the wrong way as at the top of this diagram.

CRIMP, a wave or zig-zag shape in fibres, keeps them apart and makes yarns 'lofty'. Crimp is natural in wool and applied to man-mades.

SPECIFIC GRAVITY is sometimes important. Polypropylene nets for fishermen are lighter, dry and wet, and indeed float on water. Glass fibre is three times as heavy. Wool is mid-weight and is straddled by lighter acrylics, nylon, and heavier plant fibres.

STRIATIONS or grooves along fibre surfaces add both to touch and appearance, with 'strip' filaments being as scratchy as perfectly round ones are oily smooth (Fig. 31).

We are now moving out of the technologist's world of what ought to happen and into the personal world of eye, finger tip and brain. A great many of our reactions to these variables are cultural. Some are probably not.

For example, RESILIENCE is the ability of a fabric to recover from deformation. It is the characteristic that polyesters have to stop cotton and linen getting crumpled behind the knees. This is effected by blending the optimum amounts of natural and man-made fibres. Look at the percentage indicated in your garment labels. It is normal not to want the natural drape of a fabric interfered with by such little untidy creases.

Other reactions to qualities may be learned. If a fabric looks angular and shiny, you will 'feel' with your eyes that it is stiff and scratchy. Then there is FASHION and the generation gap. Fabrics of today that seem shiny and brash to me may be perfectly serviceable. I am prejudiced against them. Why? Perhaps because I associate shininess with the

30

Fig. 31 Imagine the longitudinal views of these cross-sections. These will cause the light to be reflected in very different ways.

The cross sections in Fig. 31 are of the following fibres:

cotton	wool	silk	dacron 62 (polyester)
viscose rayon	high tenacity rayon	nylon T501	nylon, glass (meltspun)
dicel (cellulose acetate)	tricel (triacetate)	orlon S1 (fil. acrylic)	orlon 42 (staple acrylic)
vinyon (pvc pva mix)	vinylon (pv alcohol)	lycra (polyurethane)	acrilan (acrylic)

well-worn cheap suiting or 'artificial' silk that was used to make cheap blouses for brassy barmaids.

Unit building of a design, then, begins at the fibre stage. The process is now repeated though in a scaled–up manner. The microscope gives way to the magnifying glass and the good naked eye. Designers with no knowledge of chemistry can now dictate where the next variables occur. Machinery, for example, ranges from the humble spinning wheel to machines the size of cathedrals.

There are two main types of yarn – those that are made from filaments and those made from staple fibres – both products of unit building. The silkworm wraps himself in his cocoon of a double thread which oozes from two holes in his head. He is unwrapped in hot water along with a few fellows, and their gross product is made into a yarn consisting of fine long strands known as filaments.

Man's viscose rayon is made from a viscous chemical solution of

31

cellulose obtained from cotton or woodpulp. It is pumped through the minute holes in a spinneret, coagulated in acetic acid and stretched for strengthening. It can be used in the filament state or chopped into fibres, and the length of these fibres can be made the same as natural fibres. Sheep, goats and rabbits, cotton, flax, sisal and several more natural sources – even asbestos – produce usable fibres from about $\frac{1}{2}$ inch to 20 inches long. Like the molecule, most fibres, to be useful, are long – one to four thousand times longer than they are wide. Sisal is only in the ratio of 100:1 and is only used for harsh string. Man-mades can be made like natural fibres by chopping them up and treating them with machinery normally used for natural fibres.

With natural fibres and yarns there are variables which often go together. With COTTON SPINNING the fibre length is critical. With WORSTED SPINNING the fineness and the crimp of the wool fibres are the deciding factors. With WOOL SPINNING there are fewer stages. The parallelization of the fibres is less, the resultant yarn bulky and less ordered. Man-mades are made to suit cotton, worsted, woollen or linen machinery, and take on some of the respective characteristics.

Elements in these yarns may be precoloured or of different types. Once the proportion has been decided, they are normally BLENDED until homogeneous. Quantities of fibres with different qualities may be blended: polyester with cotton (strength and crease resist with comfort), or acetate with viscose, which gives a yarn which may be CROSS-DYED later (Fig. 32). This method can be used to dye contrasting tones to make a lively effect, with each fibre receiving only one dye. Cross-dyeing is economical in that a two-colour fabric may be stored undyed till a 'fashion' colour is decided. Naturally, coloured fibre or 'top' may be blended at the early blending stage, or a colour and white.

Man-made yarns in continuous filament form may be SPUN DYED. Economics necessitate large amounts of spinning fluid to be treated with colour. Both filament and fibre yarns may be dyed before fabric manufacture or, as with fibres, may be used with yarns of different dye

Fig. 33 Making optical colour by small dots.

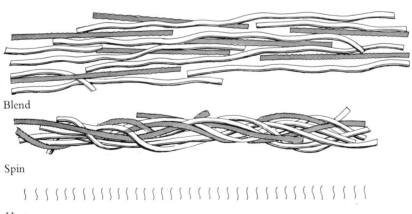

Blend

Spin

Heat

Reduce

Fig. 32 As well as colour blending, fibres with different characteristics can be spun together. After-treatment causes a new effect.

affinity. This repeats the possibilities with fibres on a coarser, more visible scale. Need I suggest the many possibilities of design by patterning areas of yarn A with yarn B, with various A and B fibre blends with a possible pre-dyed C thrown in to complicate matters? There are also dye-variant yarns where chemical modification means that the same family will dye in different tonal values in the same dye bath.

The basic process of spinning yarns may be interfered with in many ways, though perhaps a 'fancy' yarn spinner would not like his designing described that way.

TWIST: nearly all yarns need twist. Continuous filament yarns need a little to protect them in the processing which precedes and includes knitting and weaving. Much twist makes them 'crêpe' and try to undo themselves, and doing this all over a piece of fabric can produce a cockled or crêpe effect. 'S' yarns will keep on trying to undo to the left and 'Z' yarns to the right, even though they are trapped by the weave (Fig. 34).

Fig. 34 Alternate pairs of warp and weft threads are twisted in opposite directions. Because of high twist the threads will try to undo themselves, but they are trapped by the weave. This produces a lively, springy, crêpe fabric.

Twisting is vital to yarns spun from fibres. Whereas at the molecular stage strength is gained by parallelizing, at this level the fibre needs to gain friction by being crushed spirally. For decoration, bits of rubbish fibre can be fed in after the early blending. The resultant yarn goes under the delightful name of 'knickerbocker'.

DOUBLING. Having made a yarn of one thread, a whole new process begins by twisting two or more yarns together. Varying the speed of one of them causes controllable irregularities.

Much designing by unit building relies on planning ahead and thinking what subsequent processes will do to the work. Often a constant is needed. This may be regular and uninteresting in itself, but it is necessary for a variable to react with. This constancy here takes the form of smooth regular yarn, which acts as a carrier to space out the decorative spots. In music, it is the silence between sounds. The regularity is necessary to contrast the irregular decoration.

Weaving and knitting are full of instances where unit building affects the pattern. We are now dealing with sizeable units which are visible to the eye, overlapping with the more familiar areas of art.

Pointillism, or the making of optical colour by small dots (Fig. 33), a *cause célèbre* for Seurat, has been done in textiles ever since man wove his first check. The difference between Seurat and many a student is

34

that he looked and cared about seemingly small things. The student designer is rushing to the stage where he can make 'patterns'.

There are many artists today using unit-building processes in their work. One group – *Groupe Recherche d'Art Visuel* – have made a statement of their intentions which indicates that they are trying to work without using shapes that have an emotional effect. The anonymous quality is encouraged by using simple shapes repeated in sufficient quantities to create an effect on the retina. These shapes have to be big enough to make an optical dazzle and not so large that they draw attention to themselves. How near to many structural textiles!

The difference between this approach and textiles is one of motivation. Textiles decorate or keep us warm and 'respectable'; G.R.A.V. are working not to make objects so much as to create an effect on the spectator. They are using the *relationship* of one abstract form to the next in the context of art. This rules out objects that make figurative painting. The *gestalt* or total image that is presented to the eye is un-

Fig. 35 *Number 12.* Pollock, Museum of Modern Art, New York.

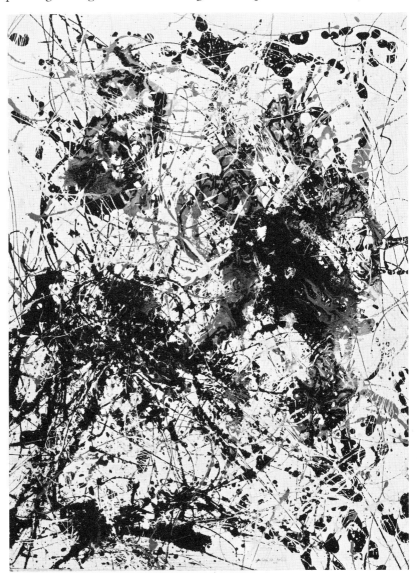

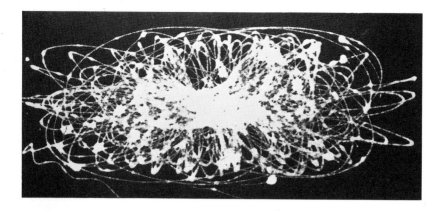

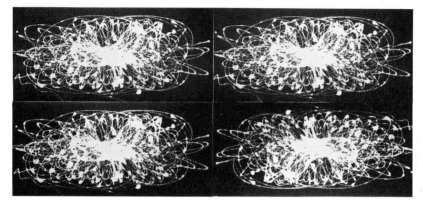

important. The G.R.A.V. artists largely use man's convention of the flat square and work from there. Against this it is easy to see which artists work within traditional compositional bounds. Jackson Pollock at first sight appears to be making over-all textures, but his activity – and activity is the operative word – is very confined to the rectangle he can reach (Fig. 35). This is very pronounced if you try to put one of his paintings into repeat (Figs. 36 and 37).

We will return to our survey of the processes of making fabric. Units of WEAVING are vertical and horizontal lines; one or the other can dominate the surface (Fig. 38). Units of WARP KNITTING are vertical and tend to zig-zag to form a joint (Fig. 39). Units of WEFT KNITTING are horizontal and are 'v' or 'u' like (Fig. 40). Units of LACE and embroidery appear to move in all directions, even appearing to curve.

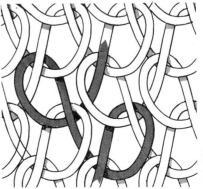

Left: Fig. 38 Units of weaving are vertical and horizontal lines. One or the other can dominate the surface.

Right: Fig. 39 Units of warp knitting are vertical and tend to zig-zag to form a joint.

36

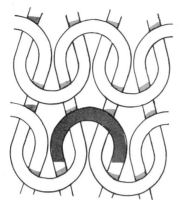
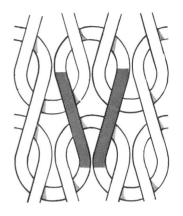

Fig. 40 Units of weft knitting are horizontal and are 'v' or 'u' like.

Above: Fig. 41 The right-angular tensions of weaving make it easy to tailor. The springy unstable nature of knitting makes it give easily to body movements.

Structurally units behave quite differently. The easiest comparison to make is that of knitting and weaving. The formation of a loop means that unequal stresses are put on the outside or inside of a loop. In weaving, the yarns are straight and may be balanced, although the warp may be under greater tension than the weft. In knitting, there must finally be a space for the needle to escape. In weaving the threads can be beaten into contact and shrunk even tighter when washed. The SPRINGY unstable nature of knitting makes it give easily to body movements. The right-angular tensions of weaving make it INERT and easy to tailor (Fig. 41). This usually means that it makes and keeps a stiffer, cleaner shape. Whether casual or formal lines are in fashion, the above generalizations still apply.

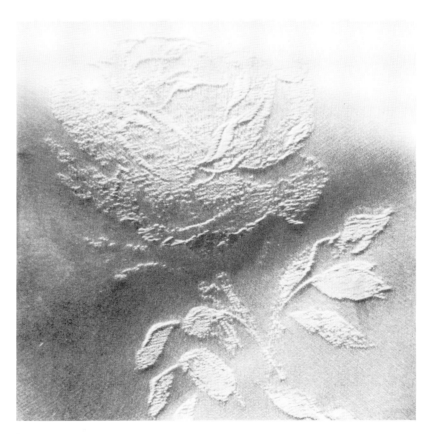

Fig. 42 In a satin the surface is of primary interest. Here a rough sketch is laboriously translated to modify the satin surface.

The interesting point about unit building is that all the build-up of linear forces of molecules, fibres and yarns, and the balancing and area making of weaving or knitting, always add up to STRENGTH. Sheet-forms of the same material could not match this strength weight to weight.

Even when people go out for the day in 'spray-on skin', there will still be scope for unit building – if only as an intellectual process.

The simplest STRUCTURE in weaving is plain weave. To make a looser, and therefore more flexible structure with the same threads, two things can be done. One is to alter the structure by 'floating' the warp or weft threads. Every time a yarn fails to intersect, it cuts out a FRICTION POINT and therefore contributes towards making the fabric flexible. Two is to reduce the number of threads. This is the cheaper procedure, and can cause troubles like SEAM SLIPPAGE when stitched.

Loosening the structure from plain weave also means that more threads may now be packed in. If these are fine and densely packed, it is possible to weave a fabric with its SURFACE as primary interest – not a pattern (Fig. 42). A duchess satin is the normal extreme, with a float length of seven. Between this and plain weave lie most fabrics.

The pattern caused by the structure in weaving or knitting is the next step in the unit-building process (Figs. 43–4). Tightness or looseness affects handle and drape. Visually there is repetition (Fig. 45). However boring this may seem to you, it often has great beauty for me. See how areas go gradually thicker or thinner when they curve (Fig. 46). See how colours gradually change. The rhythmic qualities of repetition can be beautiful, especially when broken gently by irregular yarn.

When the unit size grows bigger and it is apparent that MOTIF is the attraction, then it is important that the relationship of one unit to another is right (Fig. 47). Unit building ceases to become a philosophical point when the end-use employs one, or less than one, motif in the

Fig. 44 The pattern is caused by the structure in weaving or knitting. A pattern of squares on paper (left-hand side) is not necessarily an indication of what will happen. The marks are taken to be warp threads raised as they tradition-ally are. Here a 'honey-comb' would be designed, perhaps for a tea towel because of its large surface area. The pattern of character that we see is caused by the deep shadows formed in the 'nests'.

Fig. 43 Pattern caused by the structure in weaving.

38

Fig. 45 The beauty of repetition and rhythm, seen in furnishing repp. Each bar is waved by using two threads, each made of a hard and soft thread twisted together.

Right: Fig. 46 See how areas go gradually thicker and thinner when they curve.

Fig. 47 It is important that the relationship of one unit to another is right. Here is a knitted 8-needle jacquard by John Paul Sum showing just this.

object. Some knitwear shaped on the machine, or 'panel' printing, can partly avoid the mental processes of unit building with motifs, but in general it is inescapable.

Much of the decorative qualities of fabrics grow out of the structure (in the Bauhaus tradition), making success largely assured for people with otherwise little art sense.

This doesn't make design an easy subject. There are so many variables as I have been at great length to show. But if I have also shown that it is not just a question of 'pattern', and that design is considering what to do next and not just an afterthought, then I have succeeded.

39

Chapter 4
LIVING CANVAS

THE SHAPES OR FORMS *on the surface* of a material are what most people think of as textile design. For convenience designs are painted flat, largely made into fabric in a flat way, and often illustrated flat. It is therefore reasonable that designs tend to be thought of as flat paintings. As in painting, the shapes may be large or small, soft or jagged. This is one aspect of form – surface form – and it may be studied independently of textiles (see Figs. 48–51).

Much though I would love to, it is not the purpose of this book to dwell long on the appreciation of surface form. Here are a few simple guides which apply to continuous pattern as well as to the simple area, be it page or poster.

Above: Fig. 48 2D form becomes 3D form: a Doulton/George Tinworth vase. A vigorous band which spirals up.

Fig. 49 Almost any rubbish will pass as pattern if the basic structure is strong enough. Here nine quick sketches were made based on a diagonal square repeated at half the diagonal distance.

Fig. 50 Abstract form
inert and non-emotive,
probably does not exist.
Zig-zags can look
reptilian and spots
become eyes to warn
off!

Vertical and horizontal lines echo the world at rest. Diagonal lines
are more active when used in a pattern. Flowing lines are slow, straight
lines are quick. Uneven versions of these are livelier than even, mechanical, parallel lines, which can look cool, cold or sometimes dead. (See
Figs. 52–6.) Patrick Caulfield has made his mark as an artist by deliberately
delineating the 'art' cliché – drawing hard lines around a vase of flowers,
a romantic scene.

The structural textile designer is limited by small pattern areas.
He looks for and invents small patterns or textures which are either
visual or tactile or both. Incidentally, ask yourself at what point a pattern
is small enough to be called a texture (Figs. 57–8). By being master of

Fig. 51 Lines describing
form.

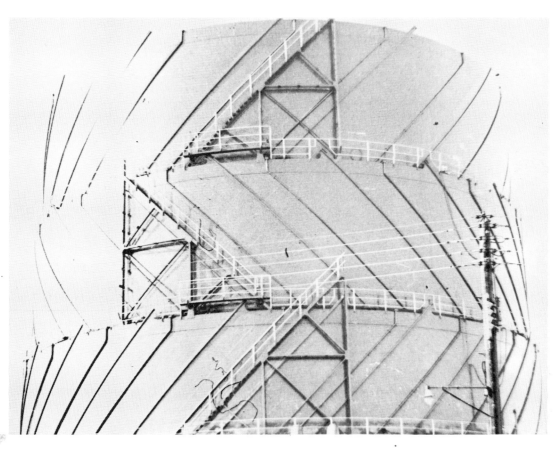

Fig. 52 Straight lines are
quick. Diagonal lines
are active.

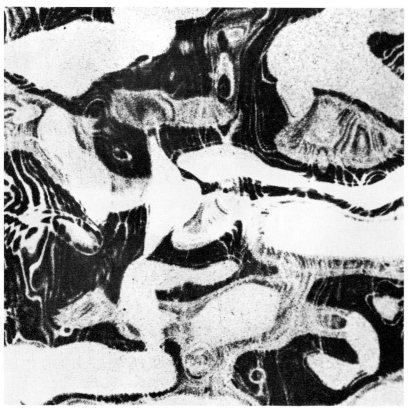

Fig. 53 Flowing lines are
slow: a negative print
of lightly disturbed
water in an indoor pool.

42

Fig. 54 A radial form.

Left: Fig. 55 A
pentagonal form.

Right: Fig. 56 An
angular form.

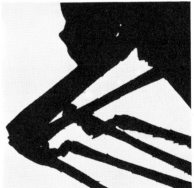

the structure, the designer is encouraged to look for and make patterns
or textures which are interesting either to the eye or fingertip or both.
Certainly one important item for students to experiment with is
rhythm: movement from one unit to the next (Fig. 59). Rhythmic
pattern is easier to produce than surface movement, which usually
requires large Jacquard machines.

Much of the formative life of a student should be spent drawing
and experimenting with shapes, proportions, textures, line and mass;
mass I would emphasize more than line (Fig. 60). Most of the teaching
of the formal aspects of surface design can be taught by an artist, but
the aim of the book is to redress the balance as I find it.

In the previous chapter I showed how small units affected the

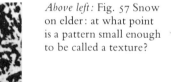

Above left: Fig. 57 Snow
on elder: at what point
is a pattern small enough
to be called a texture?

Fig. 58 Snow on larch.

Fig. 59 A single motif, picture or shape is seldom useful as a design. What is usually more important – and this becomes even more important when the motif chosen is a small one – is the relationship between the motif and the next shape. One of the effects of *positioning* is *movement*. In the illustration see how the eye travels straight up the pattern on one side and steps up diagonally on the other.

structure by a building process. Its form was determined by the way in which it was built. Taking the analogy further, the building or textile now has to be used. The architect and the builder move out. Who takes over the building? Priest or greengrocer?

The pattern cutter now plunges his shears into our precious textile. The form which the textile will take depends on his imagination and the characteristics of the textile (Fig. 61). He 'fashions' the shape round a body. At this point, however two-dimensional the thinking has been, it now becomes truly three-dimensional: the rectangle becomes a tube, the disc a cone, the concept sculpture. A fine gauzy fabric may be cut to float lightly or appear 'frothy' by gathering. A thick, coarse fabric may be cut simply to fit. The sculptor's armature is the human being. His

Fig. 60 Mass needs emphasizing.

45

Fig. 61 Often the pro-
portion of colour or
mass is considered just
as important as the
proportions of textures
together. Could there
be something in the
Victorian guide of not
mixing fur with
feathers?

preparatory drawings should either have a material in mind for exploitation or a shape for which he must find a material.

In the same way that an architect can meet the requirements of
the priest or greengrocer, so the textile designer can design for certain
broad end uses. He can, of course, perhaps produce highly original
inventions by designing both textile and garment, but the specializations
of civilization, personal aptitudes and the interest in both the two- and
three-dimensional seem to work against this.

Fig. 62 (see p. 52) shows how flat forms can be totally altered by the
way in which they are used. It shows progressive distortion of a drape with
vertical forms repeating in this order: large white, blue, large white, red.
The folds (here made into creases) have been deliberately arranged so
as to hide completely first one colour in the design and then the other.
The presence of the hidden coloured stripes is shown in a reflected glow,
referred to in Chapter 6. This by-product may not occur in curtaining,
and certainly the arranging of the drape to fit the pattern may seem
unrealistic, but it does serve to get the brain away from the 'flat picture'
idea. Practised designers will anticipate what folds will do to their flat
pictures, so one hardly ever sees a paper textile design being distorted
into folds. Students, however, should, from time to time, get involved
in making-up clothes. Having shown how a simple vertical fold changes
a design, imagine how the bumps and hollows of a human body can
distort a flat pattern. The form of the body gives clues to garment
details, for example collars for necks, and belts for waists.

The textile designer involved in narrow weaving could design
braids with such details specifically in mind. Necks, waists, collars and
cuffs will be with us after even letters have lost their serifs. They are
ways of finishing off garments and points for embellishment. In an age
when pictures, books, music and plays are appearing with no beginnings
or endings, human beings continue to pay attention to details on the
body. As that authority of fashion, James Laver, suggests, erogenous
zones will continue to shift. Fashion is here to stay – if such a contradiction
of terms is possible.

You can draw attention subtly or crudely, or choose to ignore the
shape when using surface form. The rights and wrongs of this do not
apply. These are dictated by fashion, taste and economics. Quirks of
fashion mean that normal economic rules are sometimes broken, but
usually one does not hide a complicated cut (involving extra time and
therefore money) under a complicated print (Fig. 63).

46

Fig. 64 Grass. Zebra. Same grass plus zebra.

The opposite of the above situation is the one of disguise or camouflage. The point will be quickly apparent if I mention how short, fat people soon learn not to wear black and white horizontal stripes for fear of appearing to grow sideways. In cartoons, burly burglars look even burlier in black and white stripes. This is a use of movement by line to change form.

Whereas soldiers in khaki would disappear in a summer battlefield and a zebra disappear in long grasses (Fig. 64), the weight-conscious lady can hardly pose against her matching curtains all the time (Fig. 65).

Real problems begin when you try to lose bulges on a given object. The comparative sets of discs – or near discs – arranged somewhat irrationally, show how in frontal or diffused lighting shapes lose their bulk, and how when side-lighting occurs bulk appears (Fig. 66). The

appearance of bulk is counteracted by (1) optically distracting, i.e., 'dazzling' black and white forms, (2) forms which have something in common with the bulk form (see disc with triangles), (3) disordered images, i.e., 'free' designs, or (4), mental distraction by wanting to 'read the surface' and therefore not seeing the form. This is the least likely to work consistently. Neutralization sometimes occurs. Designs made up of regular rows may confuse the bulk with their 'dazzle' but at the same time define it by making roads over every bump.

Innocence plays a big part here. It depends partly on what the brain knows. A hemisphere would be difficult to hide because the shape is simple and the eye would search for this and find it. An unknown form could be disguised more easily.

Fig. 65 Change seats?

This applies to people too. One person compliments a friend on appearing to have lost weight. A stranger walks in, and seeing her he subconsciously establishes a norm for the person based on this first encounter. First impressions are then difficult to shift. Everyone has examples of seeing things suddenly in quite a different way, which shows how deceived we are for most of our lives.

Spatial patterns and *trompe-l'œil*, i.e., patterns which appear three-dimensional, take the eye into, as well as over, the surface. Spatial patterns used indiscriminately in carpeting can be very disconcerting. No illustration can convey the uneasiness of walking across a floor which appears to have two or more levels (Fig. 67). Strangely, there are often many such effects to be found in the stores. The public seems to like glowing grids and floating curlicues – make no mistake, the public is served with some very skilful work.

Another reason why there are such designs about may be because of the designer's fascination with the effect on the drawing board. He may forget for a moment that design and indulgence in visual tricks – a part of art – are two different worlds. He should be aware at least that *looking* at a vertical design is quite a different experience from *walking* on a horizontal one.

Fig. 66 The two sets of near discs show how in front or diffused lighting shapes lose their bulk (left); with side lighting (right) the bulk appears.

Fig. 67 No illustration can convey the un-easiness of walking across a floor which appears to have two or more levels.

As the camera spawned the ciné camera, so the fascination of the aesthetics of movement grew apparent. Art galleries now creak and whirr as mini-motors strain to demonstrate some new flashing art-work under the label of 'kinetic'. Is it the gradual flicker of light from a kinetic form that makes moving water so universally fascinating? Movement and light on sequins enhance a woman's hips and make her appear either bawdy or beautiful according to time and place. Only slightly less obvious but even more difficult to illustrate is the effect of structure. Take two full-length garments, one made of thick canvas from a circus tent, the other of chiffon kerchief material. Now imagine two girls walking quickly by in these. One is almost like a mechanical doll. The jerkiness of alternate strides under the stiff cone of canvas hides her means of propulsion. Legs or wheels? The other girl swirls by. Every twitch of muscle is transmitted to the thin loose yarns which, in turn, subtly transmit energy to more yarn and long before the effect is lost, a new movement has begun (Fig. 68), modifying the earlier one and causing continuity. From the continuity comes flow and 'flowing gowns'. Between such extreme examples lie many subtle problems of usage.

Variations in handle of one per cent or two per cent are detectable

49

within the range in which particular parts of commerce work. That is to say, for example, that a suiting fabric with only a couple of threads to the inch more than another could be 'boardy' and one with two fewer would not have enough 'body'.

There are special cases where design is tied more or less critically to the fabric's use. Critical and interesting to the perfectionist are such details as thread to air space ratio in parachutes, as mentioned earlier in Chapter 1, strength and space in 'bolting' cloth sieves for flour milling and, of course, the best quality control in tyre manufacture.

It is usually more for economic than scientific reasons that the relationship of pattern to fabric is considered. Drapes may have motifs 'growing' one way, dress fabrics usually have motifs which 'grow' both ways for economical 'lays'. Even multi-directional motifs are desirable, and on a sitting-room carpet where presumably the aim is to relax, a design which flows gently around is to be preferred to one with stripes, encouraging the viewer through the room.

Cutting on the bias is a feature that may be used in tie manufacture. More importantly, this 45° reorientation of the lines of threads gives quite different characteristics to the fabric when used for dress. Similarly,

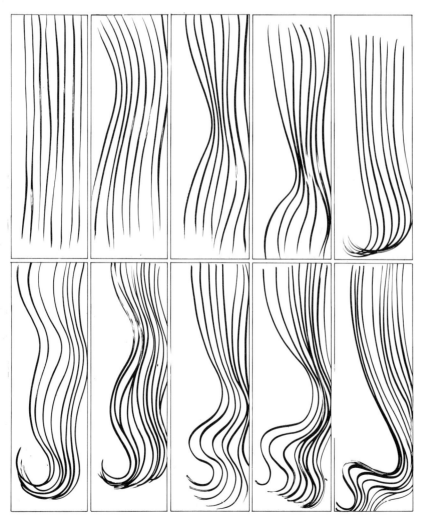

Fig. 68 Long before the effect of the first movement is lost, a new movement has begun.

Left: Fig. 69 Pattern is dependent on structure. Here a sensitive interdependence of figure, ground, rhythmic variety and machine limitations is shown by 2nd-year student John Paul Sum.

Right: Fig. 71 Stretch fabric has to be thought of as finally stretched.

other characteristics, often in themselves quite minute, affect the final form. Pattern applied as in print, or inherent as in jacquard, is dependent on structure (Fig. 69). The detail in carpet pattern is only as fine as each tuft, and is further diffused by the explosion of fibre ends as they point up from the place at which they are held (Fig. 70; see overleaf). Blankets and brushed fabrics are even more distorted, so that finicky detail is wasted, and therefore not good design.

With furniture, the beholder must necessarily be active to see, literally, the item in a different light. Its appearance is only modified by the lighting and his moving past the chair or drapery. The tautness and simple curving of furniture plays some part in the forms chosen, but because of a reluctance to regularly spend as much money the scope for expression is much less than in the fashion field.

Stretch fabric for swimwear has to be thought of as finally stretched, and all motifs should be of a shape that will not be an embarrassment to the wearer wherever they should fall in the making-up (Fig. 71).

Finally, it is worth remarking that it is easy to 'over design'. The clue to the form of the pattern may lie in the precise form of the end use. The simple structure may have a beauty which no adornment could improve and indeed would destroy.

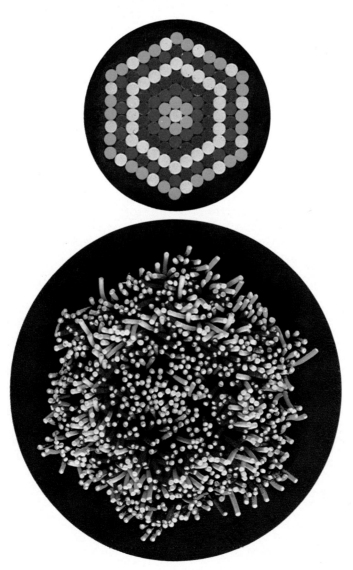

Chapter 5
ORGANIZATION THINKING

THE PROCESS OF TEXTILE MANUFACTURE is in evolution. It is easy to go into textiles and get involved in arguments about knitting versus weaving, forgetting that all known textile processes exist because no one has come up with a satisfactory way of clothing us other than with fabrics made from threads. And don't tell me you have a plastic mac!

But while I cling to the warmth of textile furnishings, my children's children may not yearn for such psychological warmth. They may be fully adapted to double glazing, strip blinds and blow-up plastic furniture. They may go out daily in a new sprayed-on skin, suitable electro-statically flocked for whatever uniform prevails or whatever is expected of their job in life.

I am not being pessimistic or cynical. New materials mean that new fabrics continue to be made, or traditional ones made cheaper and more attractive. Nylon soon became synonymous with stockings, which are both cheap and beautiful. Fashion changes are complicated by new discoveries, and revivals make possibilities endless if somewhat repetitive and similar. During this evolution there is always someone going out of business. This should never stop anyone going in. When a new discovery is made, the great technological machine has to be inched or even turned over by hand to make way for it. There is too much at stake for anyone to go out of business overnight.

In the meantime, there is more than enough scope for creativity in the established systems of organization. Digging up ancient knowledge or discovering techniques afresh can be very rewarding. Each process by its very limitation gives you a start. However nearly everyone concerned with aesthetics feels that technology fails when it tries to imitate. We have simulated leather, artificial silk, fake fur. The reasons for copying are simple enough: an expensive or unreliable original has been a good seller. Someone discovers a cheaper material that looks like the original. The market – if you can convince it that there is room for a substitute – is ready-made.

A new material not copying another – and there are many more materials invented than we see – is unlikely to be launched if the company has interests in an existing one that it would oust. Also the market might reject the new product as being too good to be true, so it might take years of careful tests and preparation of first trade and then public. Courtaulds, for example, took great care to let out its acrylic fibre, 'Courtelle', gently and slowly through haute couture in Paris. Such an approach means that it is easy to release the product, lowering the price

Fig. 72 Nature's chaos and random sprinkling of weeds is itself a form of order.

slowly. Imagine trying to upgrade a new fibre that had started life as a sacking material!

I have shown how organization is a word which applies to the big system. Organization, as I shall now refer to it, is within the textile or about the textile product (Figs. 72–4). Changing the established organization of fibre making, yarn making, cloth making, garment making and marketing would still leave most of the following ideas relevant. They are mainly based on an extension of Chapter 3, where I put forward the idea that textiles is a unit building or constructive process.

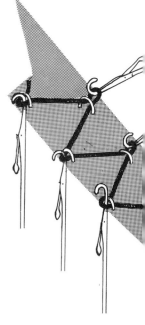

Left: Fig. 73 Man's organization often has to be ordered in a mechanical way (spinning frame).

54

Fig. 74 Spaced dyeing
and its inherent irregu-
larity combined
with regular repeating:
Bedford Cord weave by
Stephanie Elcock.

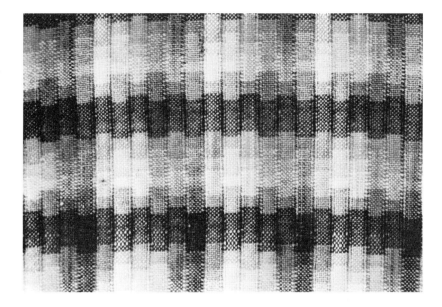

Yarn being fed in
from fixed point.

Below: Fig. 75 This
diagram shows the
simplest knitting
fabric being made.
Regard the needles as
rising and falling horses
on a fairground round-
about. They collect the
white thread as they pass
by. At the end of the
sequence (right) it is
firmly trapped. It is now
the equivalent of the
black thread at the left-
hand end of the diagram.
Now follow the course
of the black thread. The
sequence is shown as
part of a circle. In
practice this sequence is
repeated many times
round a circle of a few
inches diameter for hose
to a few feet for tubular
fabric 'in the piece'.
This particular operation
is called circular weft
knitting. The resultant
fabric from this particu-
lar sequence is plain,
such as you would do
with two needles by
hand.

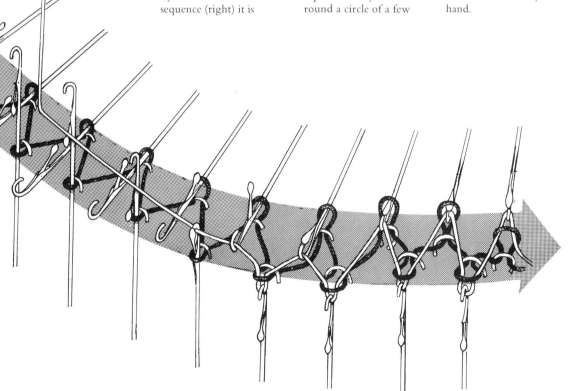

The complications of any textile machine are lessened once you realize that it is often one simple part and operation repeated perhaps thousands of times (Fig. 75). One unit is replicated. The machine unit can usually do two things, on/off, up/down, hit or miss. The unit needs to be organized. Conversely textile machinery, which usually has a master motion to operate the design of its product, is already highly organized. It is also necessarily repetitive because of the great number of units or threads that make up a useful piece of fabric. Because of this, great efforts have to be made to give variety and interest to the product – a product that easily expresses the mechanical way in which it was made. Conversely the mechanical nature of the process turns 'rubbish' into a tidy surface and slickness is made even slicker. For example, reeds which have fallen in Nature's chaos as part of a cycle towards humus, may be gathered and woven into a neat matting. Disorder becomes ordered. A bundle of plastic threads looks even more man-made when woven into a mat.

Man is probably more emotive about 'surface' than is recognized or measurable. He is undoubtedly intellectual about the surfaces he likes. When someone says 'what a super finish, how easy to clean!' you begin to wonder whether she enjoys the surface as such or enjoys the security derived from being able to tidy up meticulously.

There are 'perfect' surfaces: pristine melamines, hot pressed paper, enamel, porcelain and glass. You *know* they are reliable for the jobs they do: intellectually they score. They are continuously smooth to the touch and promise to be so over the whole area: they give subconscious security. This sensual smoothness is nothing less than sexual in its emotive content. The smoothness expresses the making process, be it moulding, baking, blowing or pressing. These make it good aesthetically.

There are other surfaces which, rough or smooth, hard or soft, warm or cold, are not expressive of the process that made them. In structural textiles almost every pleasing result comes from a mechanical unit building process *plus* necessary modification (Fig. 76). It is the modifications in making or finishing where the components are transformed into new beauty. In velvet, the unattractive loops are cut on the loom to make pile. Sometimes the visible mechanical structure is dependent on, as well as compatible with, the yarn, one helping the other to make an interesting surface.

Perfection goes hand in hand with lack of resilience, as athletes well know. The highly tuned muscle is susceptible to strain. A daisy in a bowling green is an outrage (Fig. 77). Bowling greens are designed for perfection, and flaws show more easily than they would in a lawn. Why is this? Well, not only have most lawns got a daisy or two, but they may have buttercups, plaintain, yarrow and many more obscure little bits of weeds, not to mention a variety of other grasses which make the weeds tolerable. The constant problem of a designer is to resolve a conflict of random with order, so that sufficient weeds – of the right sort – can become a feature of the lawn.

In textiles the technologist needs a yarn that is resilient enough to stand the rough and tumble of preparation, processing, knitting or weaving, finishing, and use. Filament rayons are notorious for showing every fault. Twisting these into organzines or crêpe yarns gives them a subtle irregularity and greater resilience. Not surprisingly the visual

Below: Fig. 76 Croquis (or non-repeating sketch with implications of repeating) to illustrate surface organization.

56

Right: Fig. 77 Who's stolen one of my flowers?

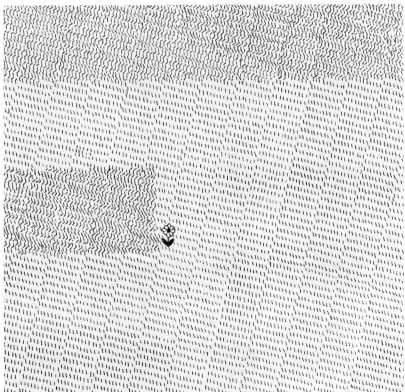

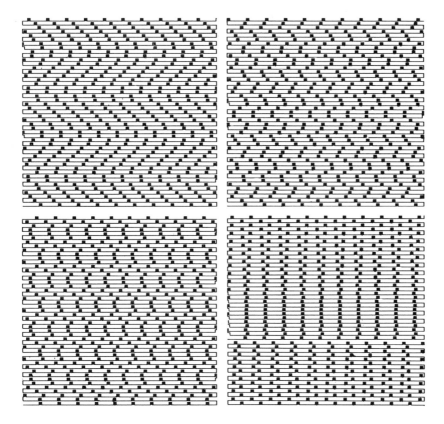

Fig. 78 Computer drawings showing four different repeating intervals. They simulate a regularly repeating feature. The slightest change of spacing manifests itself as a quite different pattern. The spaces of these are less than one per cent apart, 127, 126 and 125 units between blobs respectively. In the fourth diagram the space is 123 units in length. In this drawing the pattern has been broken at one third distance, the equivalent of changing the yarn package. This indicates the practical difficulty in making features work for you.

character is then close to yarns from natural fibres. Man may no longer need to copy natural fibres exactly, but it is salutary to note that the more successful ones have so many oddities that this is part of the overall character.

The irregularities must be organized. A piece of weaving with random weft must be organized so that the randoms don't look like mistakes. Organizing random effects in yarn is a problem which has caused much concern. I used a computer to show how a subtle change in spacing of features or faults in yarn creates a new pattern in the over-all design (Fig. 78). The blobs are regularly spaced in each case, but at different intervals. You can follow the path of the yarn backwards and forwards across the full width of the square (the fabric). The area width is constant. You can understand that (a) the pattern varies enormously for a slight change of interval, (b) a break in the line (thread) and a fresh start throws a fault line in the pattern and (c) any series of features or faults that is in any way cyclic will behave similarly. So that if the pattern is *not* to show, then the feature or fault must be a *true* random. This is a problem that continually concerns yarn users. A recent revival of space-dyed effects has resurrected the problem for new users.

In fact this is the key to it all. 'If it looks like a mistake, you've made a mistake!' When dealing with small differences you have two simple courses of action, mix or blend; all spun-yarn processes rely on this. Alternatively separate into batches. There are complicated methods of colour labelling and numbering which help to ensure this.

Let's jump to pattern organization. Pattern is a decorative embellishment which could be applied to each individual garment when it is

Fig. 79 Multi-directional unit arrangement. Mass-centred, direction-balanced and irregularly ordered.

made up, but that usually happens to be an expensive and prohibitive way of doing it. Dresses are sometimes printed in panels which, if different for each size of garment, give good control of proportion. Knitwear can be shaped by reducing or increasing the number of stitches in each row, with the pattern related to it at the same time. Embroidery may be stitched directly on to the garment or prefabricated and then applied.

The bulk of textiles are made 'in the piece' and cut out to shape. With printing it is possible to print the complete lay. Usually, though, it is understood that in both dress and furnishings there is continuity, so that a fabric can be cut to give minimum wastage. Motifs on dress fabrics go 'up' and 'down' or are multidirectional (Fig. 79). In curtaining, which will only be chopped in lengths, the motifs can 'grow upwards'. In both cases, expected seaming should be taken into consideration when designing. Some motifs need to be matched edge to edge when cut. In constructing designs one major consideration has to be met. The machine usually deals with one master pattern area, usually incorrectly known as a 'repeat', from which other areas are mechanically repeated. The eye viewing the finished object usually sees one repeat-plus. The plus can be a small part of the next repeat or several repeated areas, according to the size of repeat and the amount shown. When the pattern area ('repeat') is small, say $\frac{1}{4}$ inches $\times$ $\frac{1}{2}$ inches, with eight moves, as in an eight-needle domestic knitting machine or 8-shaft weaving, you have reached a region where the irregularities in the yarn could be as strong a feature as the pattern (Fig. 80).

Fig. 80 When the repeat is small you have reached a region where the irregularities in the yarn could be as strong a feature as the pattern. Here the irregularities become greater as you go from left to right. (Almost impossible as a realistic piece of weaving or knitting!)

Organization of pattern is closely linked to or affects structure (Fig. 81). Small structural designs can inhibit the handle and sewing qualities just because the inter-lacings are tighter or slacker. Large area designs, printed or structured, call for a feeling for the drape that will support them. The need here is for superb draughtsmanship and stylization suitable for the scale and process. Everything is on show.

Very small designs don't involve the virtuoso skill of 'drawing'. So if you can't 'draw', don't worry. But you do need to be sensitive to relationships. When repeats are small, the slightest change made to the initial pattern area is recorded faithfully again, again, again, and again. This means that in a symmetrical design you can add something symmetrically. Both designs, the first and the amended, may be satisfactory. You can argue about the merits of shape or proportion, perhaps. If, however, something is added asymmetrically, it could appear as unwanted and therefore a fault, or wanted and therefore 'perversely interesting' (Fig. 82; see p. 69).

59

Fig. 81 It is no good making designs unless the supports or structures have been thought about. The sharpness of detail in screen printing will only be as good as the fineness of mesh in the screen and the smoothness of the surface to be printed. A woven or knitted design will only be as sharp as the stitch allows and will be further affected by irregularities in the yarn. Reading down the five rows of three diagrams it will be seen that it becomes more increasingly difficult to see the shape of the white object; the detail is gradually being lost. Detail therefore should be considered relative to the material. Quality of detail is largely an 'on-off' thing. In weaving/knitting a thread is either lifted to the surface or left down. In screen printing the basic element is a gap in the mesh through which fluid is, or is not, forced.

With an initially 'free' design, however, it is almost impossible to rid yourself of either 'unwanted repeat marks' or 'unwanted lines'. Only inexperienced or insensitive designers try to put the traditional paisley-pine motif into repeats with fewer than five even motifs in the pattern area for a free flowing design. 'Even', however, is the key word. With linking elements a free design could be made with as few as two or three basically complete motifs.

Not many designers realize the fascinating usefulness of satin order arrangement. If overdone they are inhibiting. If carefully and sensibly used, they are infallible as 'column starters' (Fig. 83) or as 'mass centres' (Fig. 84). Like a crossword puzzle, a satin order has to read up and across. Only one dot shows each way. As you can see in fabric, each dot is where a warp thread comes to the surface (strictly speaking, this is a sateen effect).

The illustrations show further examples better than words. The principle which has this double use as both weave and pattern order is devised in the following way: (a) the total number of units each way are decided and marked off (5-end satin is 25 squares or 5 lines each way); (b) mark bottom left, (c) move to next row, (d) move over two columns, making a mark on the second, (e) repeat 'c' and 'd', (f) as you run to the edge go back to the beginning of the next row. This is a continuous process. You will eventually finish up with five marks in regular order, as shown in the stage-by-stage diagrams (Fig. 85). All the variations of counting are shown, from 1 to 5: (a) shows a diagonal of 'four and one twill', another weave; (b) and (c) are straightforward; (d) is like 'a' but reversed; (e) becomes a column – nonsense for this exercise.

The way to achieve satisfactory systems of a *regular* order is like this: (a) write down the figures involved – 1, 2, 3, 4, 5; (b) cross off last, 5; (c) cross off twill makers (1 and 4); (d) cross off any other figure that

Fig. 85 Regular 5-end satin.

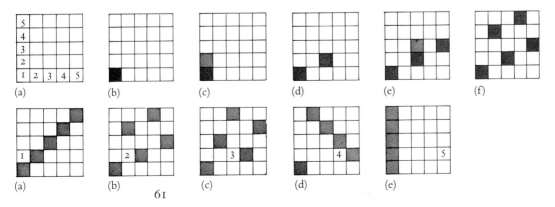

has a measure with the total (in this case there are none left). Now we'll try it with the other most used satin, the 8-end: (a) 1, 2, 3, 4, 5, 6, 7, 8; (b) 1, 2, 3, 4, 5, 6, 7, x; (c) x, 2, 3, 4, 5, 6, x, x; (d) x, x, 3, x, 5, x, x, x; (e) use 3 or 5. Try out the principle and it provides four variations. Try one of these and repeat the weave each way, up and across, making four repeats in all. I expect you will have noticed that all the marks fall in diagonal lines. If you devise an *irregular* method much of the lining disappears.

Unless you are a mathematical genius, the method for *irregular* satins is a little hit-and-miss, but it is on these lines: (a) mark off the total as before; (b) mark the bottom left; (c) move to the next row; (d) move over 'n' columns making a mark; (e) repeat 'c' and 'd' to *halfway* up the area; (f) count one half of the total instead of 'n' – just once, then (g) move over 'n' *to the left*; (h) continue to finish.

In the larger satin orders the count number 'n' can be two alternating figures. All the steps for an 8-end irregular system are illustrated (Fig. 86), as are 6, 10 and 12 systems (Fig. 87). Finally, the 6 is modified, which

Fig. 86 All the steps for an 8-end irregular order.

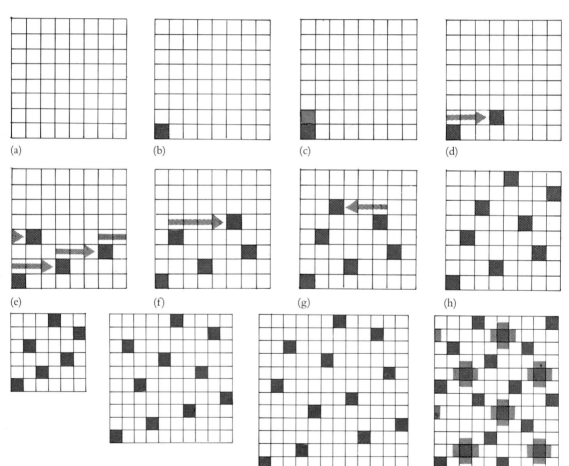

(a) (b) (c) (d)

(e) (f) (g) (h)

Fig. 87 6, 10, 12-end irregular systems with a 6-end with additions to make two sizes of areas.

shows how to use satins as a starting point.

But we have become so inhibited about even numbers in weaving that the 'awkward' 7-end satin is almost unheard of. I only discovered it for myself in writing this. The 7-end satin is awkward in practical terms so everyone forgets it. The following reference to figures gives

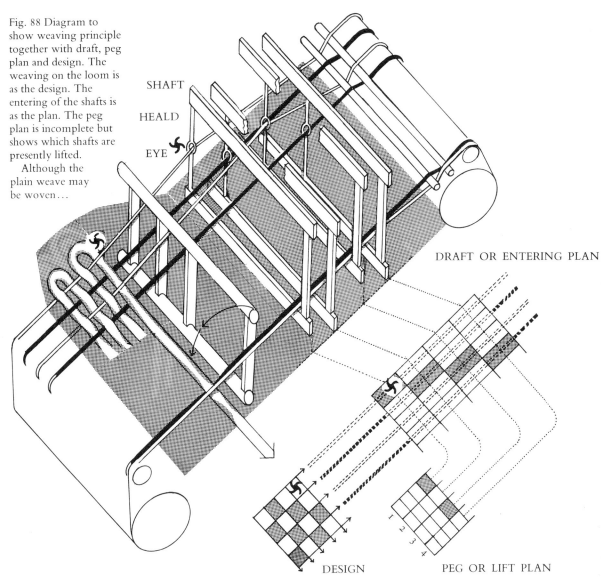

Fig. 88 Diagram to show weaving principle together with draft, peg plan and design. The weaving on the loom is as the design. The entering of the shafts is as the plan. The peg plan is incomplete but shows which shafts are presently lifted.

Although the plain weave may be woven...

SHAFT

HEALD

EYE

DRAFT OR ENTERING PLAN

DESIGN

PEG OR LIFT PLAN

on a fixed heddle (sheet punctured alternately with slots and eyes), or two shafts, it is convenient – because the heald is thicker than the thread – to spread out the threads over four shafts. For plain weave you then regard 1 and 3 as linked and 2 and 4 as linked. The exploding here makes rather a bitty diagram. However you can see the shed lines referred to in the text. Top shed is presently white, bottom shed black.

some indication why this is so and how the practical side of the process is inhibiting.

In all weaving a fixed heddle or two shafts are the minimum requirements. The warp is divided into 'shed' lines while a shuttle is passed through. The simplest form that this can take is plain weave. Odd threads are on top for the first shuttling across, while even threads are down; then the position is reversed for the second passage of the yarn-carrying shuttle. As the healds that hold the warp threads take up more room than the threads, it becomes convenient to spread out the threads over four shafts instead of two (Fig. 88). You then regard one and three as linked and two and four as linked. Logically there is little to be gained by adding two more shafts, so the next 'useful' number is eight. Sixteen follows as the normal limit for hand looms.

Design paper is ruled in columns and lines (though you may see them as squares) which are collected together in groups of eight. Weavers very soon become octavists. Or is it octophiles?

Grouping tends to make weavers think that colour should fit neatly into eights or at least into the weave repeat, and of course it is very convenient to construct with numbers that are easy to remember. While I criticize students for lacking originality, I am aware that some of the most beautiful designs in the world are the sole designs that their weavers know. Peasant weavers learn *the* design from their fathers, number by number, weave it all their lives, and pass it on to their children; a case of 'practice makes perfect', a different example of which is shown in Fig. 89. There are many books on how-to-do-weaving with romantic names for weaves that can be done this way, and they tend to back up this type of thinking. A weaver does not need encouragement to fall into formulae. It is easy to tidy up and rationalize numbers so much that you forget to put trust in your eye. Ultimately the eye is the judge, and if something looks right it probably *is* right. Apart from that, your work goes stale if you forget to delight your eye in looking and enjoying. Your mind goes blank, your shapes go sterile and there is a visual and mental tightness in general.

Fig. 89 A painting on silk by an unknown Japanese artist. He probably used special brushes – a 'fur' brush, a 'bamboo' and a 'whisker' brush – a celebration of 'practice makes perfect'.

Fig. 90 Forms designed multi-directionally.

This is a good place at which to make the point that thinking, bogged down by a process, is on a par with thinking that is bogged down by another technique.

There is an arrogance about students who have had a little success in another branch of art. Usually it is related to linear drawing in some way. A degree of cleverness is reached in making marks. These marks are special to the techniques, whether they be dots and dashes of ink, flourishes of the brush, regular stylo lines or virtuosity with an HB pencil. If their success is dependent on their slick use and no more, then you have a useless designer in the making. Well, not quite useless, as being clever enough to learn one technique may mean that he or she will be clever enough to learn another.

When the translations of the artist's marks are successful, they can be very effective indeed. The technologist, of course, should take the credit that is due to him, which brings up the argument about 'idea' that is enlarged in Chapter 8. Any mark that an artist can make is capable of interpretation but poses the question 'Does the technologist know what the artist wants interpreted?' If he makes a mistake, he has failed from the artist's point of view.

Alternatively the technologist may see something interpretable in an artist's (throwaway) work. Isn't the technologist now the ideas man? Much of designing is knowing *how to stylize* and what to select to use. Perhaps I am being over modest when I say that designs can be spat out, but selectivity is very important.

So, would-be designers of structural textiles – remember to use the systems and machinery of organization. Don't let it use you. Drawing is clever, but it must contain the right ingredients. Drawing from something out of life will keep you alive. 'Drawing' is the manual skill that graphic artists should maintain.

The three illustrations in Fig. 90 show the dangers of systems in repeating designs. The half-moon design shows an object rotating in lines both vertically and horizontally (shaded areas indicate the first repeating line in each direction). This causes unwanted diagonal lines and dark and light bands. It is arguable that these faults are positive enough in this case to allow the design to be useful. Indeed it may be thought that this is good. Much creativity in design lies in knowing when to recognize that an accident may be preferable to the intended line of thought. Try not to be inhibited by technique, habit or safety so that such an effect passes unnoticed. However as my aim would be to encourage the designer to gain *control* of the elements he is working with, be it form, tone, movement or colour, a solution is offered by starting each rotational run successively in positions 1, 4, 7, 2, 6, 3, 8, 5. This gives a balanced all-over multidirectional design so desirable for economic cutting when 'making up'. The 'moon' illustration shows the effect of filling out the shape to give a rough but carefully controlled spot. The numbering order is slightly different, but as before there is only one spot facing the same way in any line or row. This is no accident as this pattern system is derived from a structure in weaving which must necessarily work. It is an '8-end irregular satin weave'.

Chapter 6
COLOUR

MANY ARTISTS, DESIGNERS AND TEACHERS seem to feel that to theorize about colour is like theorizing about love – it takes away the magic. Some say you can't teach anyone to be a good colourist. You're a have or have-not. I will reserve my opinion, at least until I have discovered what is a 'good' colourist.

First we must look for a constant. Some people say there is no such thing as a good colour scheme. I wonder if it is a self-indictment that I have lived through one period of fashionable colour going 'yuk' to the dreary colours that rage triumphant? Is good colour the one that I like myself?

What do I see if I am colour blind? Some of the answers come from studying books about colour theory. See what they have in common. Don't be put off by unattractive or old-fashioned illustrations. These show how ideas change. Probably you may think their results unexciting. The answer to this is the same as in life itself. Once you have found order and a cosy way of life you will need something different, something which breaks the rules. Later in the chapter I will make my contribution to some rules which are made to be broken.

How important is colour in textiles? Almost always it is the 'right' colour that will sell the slightly inferior fabric. You are attracted from a long way off by the 'right' colour. Your reasoning powers are attacked by an emotional feeling of like or dislike on first sight. People are less aware of other aesthetic factors such as 'visual texture' or 'handle'. You could buy the 'right' colour but not even notice whether the fabric was knitted or woven.

Just as colour is usually the one most important factor, so it is the easiest to change. A company may spend weeks or months doing market research, having yarns specially spun, material made, all the processing problems smoothed out, production runs produced, finished, finalized and costing accounted. Then who decides on the colour? Is it the designer? It could be the managing director or he could turn to his secretary, or Tom, or his two friends Richard and Henry, who could breeze in and suggest a new colour.

Strangely enough, it is quite often easy to change the colour even at this late stage. After all, colour usually makes no difference to performance in the manufacture and it doesn't make the fabric thicker or thinner. It is often as easy to dye a yarn or fabric in one colour as it is in another. And it could take less than a minute to change the colour on a knitting machine or loom. So the most influential textile factor is at

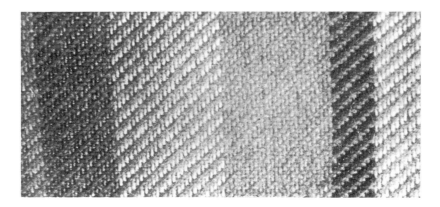

the mercy of anyone. What then is the 'right' colour?

First from the giver's point of view. The right colour from the commercial viewpoint is the one that sells the goods. What is right today could be wrong tomorrow. This means you were too late with your fashion. Conversely you can be too early, too! The right colour is the popular choice of the body of people whom it interests or for whom it was designed. (Marketing may have to take into account that a choice is offered in order to sell only one colour.)

In England black is 'right' for a funeral and yet in Southern Italy or Malta white is correct for the same sombre event. Such cultural reasons may be many, conscious and subconscious, affecting what must be offered. Superimposed on cultural, regional and climatic requirements is 'pure fashion' – the natural desire for change.

Now the recipient's point of view. The second right colour is the one that suits *you*, the customer. Your choice may vary according to context. Very reasonably you may prefer candy coloured dresses, deep rich colours in furnishing, brown and cream 'wholesome' colours in food, bright plastic utensils and neutral colours in metallic gadgets. Yet if someone asked you your favourite colour they would be talking in abstract terms and you might answer 'red' in the same spirit. These are the colours that go to dictate your life-style or personality.

The third 'right' colour is for the successful designer who can put his own likes and dislikes where they belong. This can vary according to his market. A 'one off' or short run designer will be selling at least some of his goods because of his distinctive style and colour. The same designer might be like a fish out of water in a company making long runs and selling to a large number of people.

When this is done, cost saving is keener. A small number of colours and designs are made and moved in large quantities. A wide range of colours in anticipation of a customer only makes the shelf bigger. Stock on the shelves is money locked up. Ultimately the customer pays for the service of choice, so to keep it cheap the designer is forced to work with a few 'right' colours. This throws the emphasis on to careful market research with possible computer aid, remembering to feed the computer properly first. Alternatively there is the usual route of experience, 'knowing your market' and having hunches.

There are many other occasions where there are 'right' colours. The problems begin in earnest as soon as colour is taken seriously by educators. Colour taught in a technological environment will tend to be quite different from that taught in an art school. Technologists, by definition, look for method and formulae in the industrial arts. Colour may even appear as a ten-day package with a certain amount of information which is opened, shown to the student, and then wrapped up and put on one side as done.

Art by tradition is a skill. At worst this means that colour will be taught on a how-to-do-it basis. This may on the surface seem preferable to many of the apparently useless activities that go under the label of art, but in fact it means that colour will be introduced as an important though not essential element of visual expression and communication.

The medieval emphasis on learned skills has gradually been shifted aside and the creative process is now on top. Art education is a guidance, a widening of horizons, which often draws heavily on the other senses and highly intellectual forms. The experience of involving the spectator is played on. Colour may be pointed out as an avenue to pass along for its own sake, and may (or may not) crop up as an important ingredient in other creative work.

To over-simplify, the right colour for the technologist is the one that comes from the rule book of an accepted theorist. Conversely, the right colour for the artist is one that breaks all known rules, is reminiscent of no one else's colour, and is the only one that would work on the artifact that is on show.

In design education I suggest elsewhere three elements: awareness, control and detachment. Control is a matter of practice, natural flair and discipline. By detachment, I am referring to the part that comes later when there is an awareness of others' problems and some control of them. Awareness is a continuous process starting before college and, I hope, carrying on long after. To make students aware of colour you can let them discover it by presenting the right projects, and support them with some supplementary information. I shall now introduce such information, which concerns the physical, physiological and psychological aspects of colour.

Colour in textiles can never be treated in the abstract. It is inextricably linked with the character of the yarn. The yarn, in artists' language, is the 'support' or canvas on to which the painting is done. But whereas a canvas, apart from 'tooth', is an inert surface supporting some vital activity, the yarn may be highly charged with qualities inherent in its chemistry and physical make-up. Knitting, weaving and finishing develop these further. Silk, for example, when printed, has a sheen and accepts and reflects very subtle shades: cotton printed with a similar design may turn out very dull. To give it 'life' a whole tradition of designs has been built up whereby little white areas and sometimes black outlining are used on cotton.

Physically light has a particular character according to the occasion. It falls on the textile which rearranges it and sends it up for our eyes to see. Painters will appreciate the action of light and material. A tomato on a piece of white paper lying under a blue sky is like a radio receiver. But whatever waves it picks up, it absorbs everything with the exception of red, which is transmitted to our eyes. But anyone who believes this and now tries to make a realistic painting by saying 'Ah, it's red and a sphere – a sphere is sort of light at the top and dark at the bottom' is in for trouble.

Fig. 82 Adding or missing out a part of a motif on a small repeating design is recorded again, again, again, and again. Any stage of a symmetrically built design could be used as a design in its own right. Parts added or missed asymmetrically, although enlivening, are recorded faithfully again, again, again . . . They could appear as unwanted, and therefore a fault, or wanted and therefore 'perversely interesting'.

The shiny surface does not allow such simplicity. It makes a weak, crudely spherical mirror which collects and distributes the blue sky as a purplish area and the sun as a bright white spot. It casts a coloured shadow. It may even reflect into the shadow. When your friend arrives in a yellow shirt, one side of the tomato goes towards orange. But what do *you* see? Both eye and brain are involved.

Physiologically what you see depends on your personal equipment and how you use it. We have five million cone-shaped receptors, mostly grouped in 1/180th part of the back of the eyeball, the foveal region. These give us the ability to see colour. This delightful sensation is not for cats or dogs, but the birds and the bees have something to whistle and hum about. One in ten males is markedly confused by red and green, and many more have lesser degrees of deficiency. This occasionally means that one of the cone systems is missing, but usually colour 'blindness' means no more than reduced sensitivity to some colours.

The eye, along with man's inventions of television and today's colour films, uses red, green, and (violet) blue. They are the primary colours when dealing with additive colour. It takes a bit of believing that lights of these colours, when added together, make white light.

A few artists preoccupy themselves with work that emphasizes the physiological sensation of seeing – working on the eye with so-called 'optical' effects. They all rely on the brain (but not necessarily the intellect) to do something about the information that the eye transmits to it.

The physical deals with the nature of light, the inorganic; the physiological area, like a second receiver/transmitter, allows *you* to see and is considered organic.

Psychologically light reacts through the brain. It is not until you begin to paint something realistically that you realize how much detail you normally miss. The brain uses the eyes to give us only as much information as we need to know. Our 'seeing' of the tomato in the sun in the second or two before realizing that it *is* a tomato is probably much more acute than it would be if we were casually told 'Look at that tomato!' 'Oh, yes,' we'd say and look away.

But the ability to see *freshly* often only works up to the point when the object is recognized. The brain searches through its filing cabinet and finds the picture of a previously-seen tomato. To get there it may have said 'I'm looking for something red, shiny, and round', and very soon hazards a guess. As a tomato on a piece of white paper in the open air is slightly unusual – even mildly surreal – our eyes and brain may just give it slightly more attention than usual – measured in microseconds if you like! But again we say 'Oh, yes, a tomato!' However the painter is dealing with the inherent qualities that make the tomato look real. The layman-painter knows his painting is not quite right. But it may take some while before he *perceives* the pale purple and orange caused respectively by the blue sky and the yellow shirt.

Eye and Brain by R. L. Gregory and *Art and Illusion* by E. H. Gombrich (see Further Reading), deal at length with the effect of what we know on what we see. Professor Gombrich quotes Roger de Piles in 1673 on the bad habits of painters whose 'eyes see the objects of nature coloured as they are used to painting them'. This is an indictment of artists of any age who either work to a formula or forget to renew their observations of the world. Optical illusion is one thing, difficult to fight in spite of yourself. Self-delusion or laziness is another.

One morning, when I was a love-sick youth, a sound at 8 a.m. made me peer through the brown October chestnut leaves to see the postman's red van. The promise of a letter made me see a piece of bright red van. I stared in disbelief as the 'red' faded 'in front of my eyes' into a dull brown leaf and swung, idly mocking.

As with other subjects the teaching of colour relies on the recurrence of relevant points. The ultimate way of learning how to apply colour to textiles is to do it. Awareness at the beginning of a student's life is perhaps limited to self-taught facts about personal colouring. Mid-grey-blue contrasts well with blond hair, does things for blue-grey eyes and makes the skin seem healthily tanned. But a favourite textile, as we have seen, may be made up of many complicated components. In no time at all students can be brought to the point of producing textiles. The results will be what they like, and often they will delude themselves into saying that the results are what they intended. In fact the variables, particularly in weaving, are numerous. They defy a *fully* predetermined result to the most imaginative and experienced designer. Thus unless there is a project – e.g. colour from nature to interpret or a range of colour ways for a known market or other specified project – it is difficult to assess a student's progress in awareness and control of colour. Discipline needs to be imposed, either by the teacher or the student – preferably by the student under guidance.

Many books on colour deal with colour in abstract terms but with paint or ink in mind. Textiles have many characteristics which make the application and effect of colour unstraightforward and difficult to illustrate. For example, yarn is made of fibres which may each be of separate colours (Fig. 93; see overleaf). Yarn may be knitted or woven in single units (threads). Blue and red used this way would make an optical purple (Fig. 94; see p. 76). In a printed textile, areas of the same blue printed over the same red would produce a different, duller purple, brown or near black. This shows one effect of the 'positioning' of colour. The amount, too, is important. Equal amounts of the right and balanced red and blue will give purple, but varying the proportion will affect this.

If this sounds obvious, consider that an unsure student will often fall into the trap of asking 'Do these colours go together?', holding up two packages of yarn. This brings up a third point very frequently overlooked or barely mentioned in the most long-winded discussions on colour systems – that of scale, viewing distance and viewing angle. Many of these effects are in turn linked to another point which is not yet clear. The effect, however, is well known.

Where there are two areas of equal interest, your eye seems to go backwards and forwards from one to the other, yes-no, yes-no, on-off. It is easy to be disturbed by this arrangement, which is easily associated with the flickering effect which disastrously upsets epileptic sufferers (Fig. 95, see p. 77). If the eye scans a surface which is made of hundreds of these double areas, then it is not surprising that it soon gives up and accepts a mixture – or is it an average? For example, a piece of plain weaving with red warp and blue weft threads can be seen as such when close but becomes too much of a problem when seen at a distance. At the same time a coarser fabric or bolder pattern will need to be taken further

Left: Fig. 92 Nature makes harmonies of colour. The emphasis can change hour by hour. The three out-of-focus studies here show both the difficulty and excitement of using nature's colours.

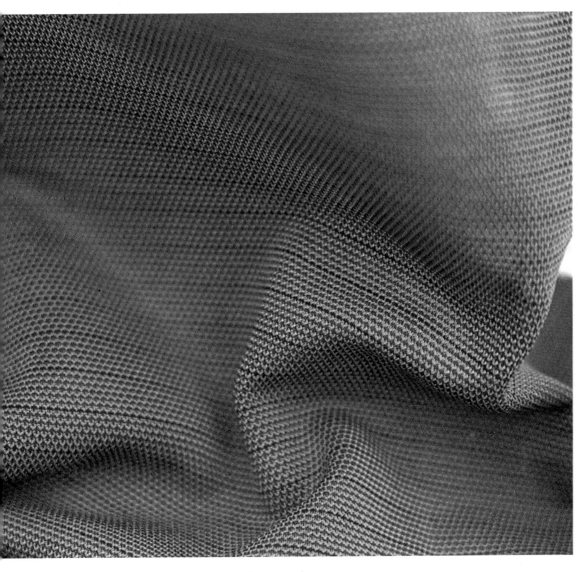

Above and right: Fig. 93
Optical grey made from
multi-colour
components.

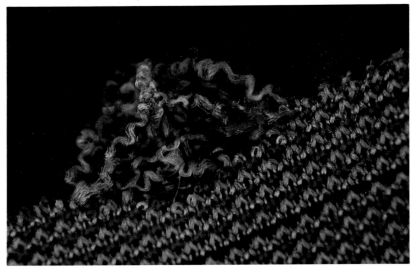

73

away before the same effect occurs (Fig. 96). You will then be making the image of the second fabric on your retina the same size as the image of the first one.

Narrowing the angle reduces the apparent size of one of the two dimensions of a pattern (Fig. 97). Several factors help this two-colour effect and two colours can be used in several ways. One is repetition, presumably suggesting to the brain that it is not worth continuing with the study. Colours made this way are more interesting than single colours (Fig. 98, see p. 77). Secondly, the ordered nature of the arrange-

Fig. 96 A coarser fabric or bolder pattern will need to be taken further away to appear the same size on the retina. Conversely, the colours in a near pattern appear different when the pattern is taken further away.

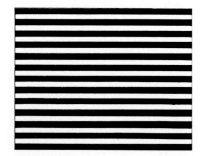 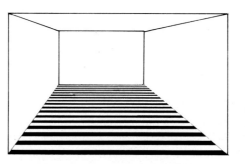 

ment. This is not so much for its monotony or boringness but as a board of constancy from which to spring surprises. Consider an analogy in movement. When I was a boy I used to think that some aircraft in films were standing still in the air. Often there were sequences where the film makers forgot, or were unable, to put in clouds for 'reference' and, of course, the camera travelling beside the filmed plane gave no sense of speed. The use of a constant allows you to be surprised when something else happens to interfere with the overall order. Many systemic painters use a grid as a base. A third factor, usually more quickly discovered, which enhances the effect of pairs of colours used optically, is the balancing of values. Ambiguity of figure and ground interest relies on two colours. Though many of the points I refer to are dependent on two *forms*, a ground (like white paper) and a figure (like black line drawing), they are enhanced by the two 'right' colours. This works particularly well with ambiguous figures where the figure is the ground and then the ground the figure. Using more than two colours does not often improve this effect.

Fig. 97 Narrowing the angle reduces the apparent size of one of the two dimensions of the pattern. A carpet, left, when viewed, may appear as in the centre diagram. To stop you making spatial assumptions I have isolated and inverted the three-dimensional carpet image. It emphasises the great change that has come about in the image that is projected on to the retina.

74

The exciting point about colour is that you can go on learning about it and indeed there is still room for research by would-be theorists. I have made one modest discovery unpublished, I think, by anyone else which shows how even 'abstract' shapes like squares and stripes can present us with surprises (Fig. 99, see p. 81). The predictability of the effect of other colours on the beholder is even more complicated when 'shapes' are involved. An abstract is never *pure*. An orange disc could remind a cold person of the sun, a child of a sweet and a greengrocer of work. Because of the very context of this book you'll say, 'It is a colour exercise, it's supposed to do something!'

I must now undo one or two knots which have served to strangle art students of recent decades. Well-intentioned efforts to get students to avoid the safety of harmonies of analogous, triadic and dominant colours have meant that such effects have been completely overlooked when they could have been learned and shelved as stand-bys. Simple harmony, for example, is inherent to structured textiles. When you look at any one-coloured textile you will see the dyed colour plus shading due to the three-dimensional nature of the yarn and structure. You may think you are looking at texture but in reality it is a range of values of the colour.

If you want a livelier one-colour textile you cheat a little and dye the components first, separately. A 'one-colour' textile of two yellows, two oranges or, more obviously, yellow and orange presents beautiful subtleties when the textile folds. When more contrasting colours are used it is more commonly known as a 'shot' effect – the warp is crossed with 'shots' of the weft (Fig. 100, see p. 80). Flat tonal value harmonies make invaluable printed effects called '*camaieux*' which, if a little ordinary in textile form, give the initiative to the dress designer. ('False' *camaieux* effects are more lively. Here the hue shifts as well as the tonal values, as with spirals or diagonals simultaneously on two planes in a colour solid.)

Dominant colour harmonies are an everyday necessity. Nearly every fabric producer offers alternative colourways from two to twenty, but usually four or five. If you take pink roses and grey-green leaves on a white ground to be one colourway, what are the alternatives? Well, they could be blue roses and yellow-grey leaves on white, orange roses and turquoise-grey etc. There is no strict rule or hard logic, but it is fairly easy to see that in this case the flower is bright and the leaves a greyed complementary.

The general feeling or mood of the colourways offered to customers is similar. If I decided to colour the white ground on one colourway, I would need an extra process which would not only make this a more expensive fabric to make (and someone would pay) but it might sell less because I would have effectively reduced the *expected* choice.

Dealing with colourways where there is an obvious bias is fair business. But how about when the original design is made of equal amounts of red, yellow and blue, all gloriously bright – or, equally, all deadly dull? (Fig. 101, see p. 80.) You can change around the areas of colour, but I doubt if it would offer a reasonable choice. The solution lies in the use of the maligned dominant harmony where one hue is a base and the pattern uses further colour or colours to enhance it. Conversely, further colour or colours are used and shapes are found to support them. There are nine different principles of harmony and many

Above : Fig. 95 Flickering
effect caused by repeti-
tion and close values.

Right : Fig. 98 Colours
made this way are more
interesting than single
colours.

Left : Fig. 94 Blue and
red used this way make
an optical purple.

more implicit according to the theorist Albert Munsell, whose work was published in 1921. A distillation of his findings is that harmony came from an ordered relationship of parts. For example, there would be a harmony found in light, mid, and dark colour when the steps were even to the eye. Similarly in the steps from bright to dull and from hue to hue.

It is in fact possible to have steps through all the three-colour dimensions at once! Who can deny the validity of these harmonies when flowers and plants that we cherish often contain all of them. I am assuming that you are not a harassed housewife who is hooked on the 'idea' of having flowers bought her, nor a student who is reacting against flowers as a symbol of conservatism, domesticity and 'taste'.

Munsell's system of colour notation, better explained in diagrams, is good in that it hits home the three dimensions of colour (Fig. 102, see p. 84). It is good in that it tries to do away with vague terms, although there are times when I would rather feel the mood of a descriptive 'plum' in a fashion report than read 'Dior's favourite colour this year seems to be 5RP5.5/4' and dutifully turn up my references. A buyer in New York, however, could phone 5RP5.5/4 to London and have some goods precisely dyed. To do this, the necessary requirements are accurate colour matching by both parties to identical references, in identical lighting. Accuracy is understood. References mean that they each have a book of colour samples. The same light is equally important. The simple reason for this is that some colours are metameric, and therein lies a snag. It is possible to match two chocolate browns in daylight. Brown 1 is dyed with dye A, Brown 2 is dyed with a mixture of dye B and dye C. All right so far. But when you take the samples under a lamp any one of the dye components may respond differently and shift the colour to khaki.

The rest of this chapter is taken up with a glossary of terms often found in colour as related to textiles. I finish with a chart of possible synonyms which show some of the confusion. I would plump for the theorists' list as a list of constant terms, although even theorists vary. Theorist, physicist, dyer, painter and fashion writer are all interchangeable. The terminology is confusing and language roots do not help. I had a South American student who for days was confused because 'tonos' in Spanish means 'hue'.

The meanings of words are inconstant, as popular usage causes change. I have tried to explain the current use of terms in a chart of synonyms. Here are some more definitions as I understand them.

Additive colour: a theorist's term for colours made by adding one coloured light to another or others, putting together again the component colours of light. Red and green make yellow; then add violet-blue to make white, or 'all-colour'. Alternatively mix red and violet-blue to make magenta; then add green to make white, etc.

Analogous: neighbouring, close-to, usually refers to hues.

Bastard colour: automatic by-product necessary in some processes of making wanted colour samples, e.g., a red, green, purple warp in sections is crossed by a red, green, purple, weft in turn (in sections).

Red crossing red, green crossing green, purple crossing purple, are 'true' colours. All other results, e.g., red weft crossing green warp, red weft crossing purple warp etc. are bastard colours.

Colour blanket: a series of colour trials of a textile made at one time.

Colourway: one of two or more colourings of a design offered to a customer. Each component colour in a colourway enhances the bias of that colourway.

Complementary: red has blue-green to complement or make up all-colour (black/grey) in pigment; red has blue-green (cyan) to make all-colour (white/grey) in light. (See Fig. 103, see p. 85).

Fast and fugitive: fast colours fasten themselves to their support. Dyes can be 'fast' to strong light and also to seawater, washing, perspiration and rubbing. Dyes and paints which fade quickly are termed 'fugitive'. Bright pinks, lemons and turquoise (see primaries) can be fugitive in some forms. Consult relevant literature on 'fastnesses' or 'permanence'.

Induced colours: effects brought about by combining certain kinds of colours in certain kinds of arrangements. The individual colour messages become confused in the eye and brain, resulting in colour changes directly related to mixtures of 'coloured' light. Also known as 'optical colours' (Fig. 104, see p. 85).

Optical colours: see 'induced'.

Primaries: colours which cannot be obtained by mixing other colours. In light they are red, green and violet-blue. In paints and dyes, *if* reduced to three, the most versatile are the brightest, magenta pink, yellow, and cyan (turquoise) blue. Hickethier uses these as horizontal cornerstones for his cube which is suspended by its white corner. Munsell chose ten major hues: red, yellow-red, yellow, green-yellow, green, blue-green, blue, purple-blue, purple and red-purple. R, Y, G, B, P are principal hues; YR, GY, BG, PB, RP are intermediate. They adapt well to decimalization! Psychologists consider that our response to colour shows that red, yellow, green and blue are primaries.

Simultaneous contrast: the positioning of colours so that they are seen together and affect each other.

Spreading effect: induced effect when two colours are mixed visually causing apparent changes.

Subtractive (see also additive) pigment or dye mixes: all white light is absorbed except for the colour we see. Adding all pigments or dyes together results in the taking away of all white light into them leaving black (in practice dark grey).

Successive contrast: studying a colour or tonal patch or living in a coloured light will cause 'fatigue' of the retina and the retina adapts to its new

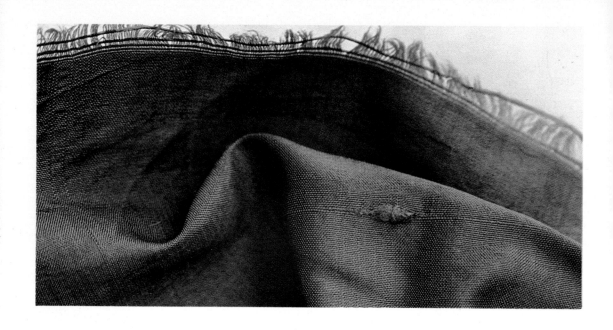

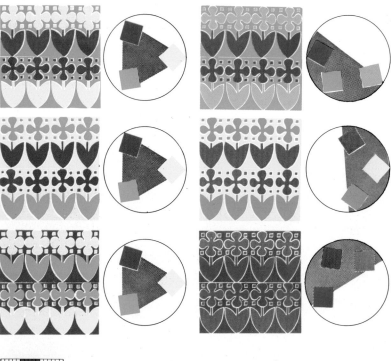

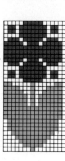

Fig. 101 This coloured
diagram shows the
difficulty with a design
of a triadic arrangement
of equal areas of colour.
Offering three colour-
ways with blue, yellow
and red grounds could
give nothing more than
a re-arrangement. From
a distance all designs
could appear optical
grey and depending on
context at close quarters
could be seen as
different designs. A
positive, if sometimes
mundane, solution is to
shift the component
colours towards the
ground colour. The
inset shows the propor-
tion of each colour by
squares. It also shows,
incidentally, the effect of
a unit limitation that
might be met with in
structural textiles, where
a shape is mirrored on 8
columns and runs
straight up 32 lines.

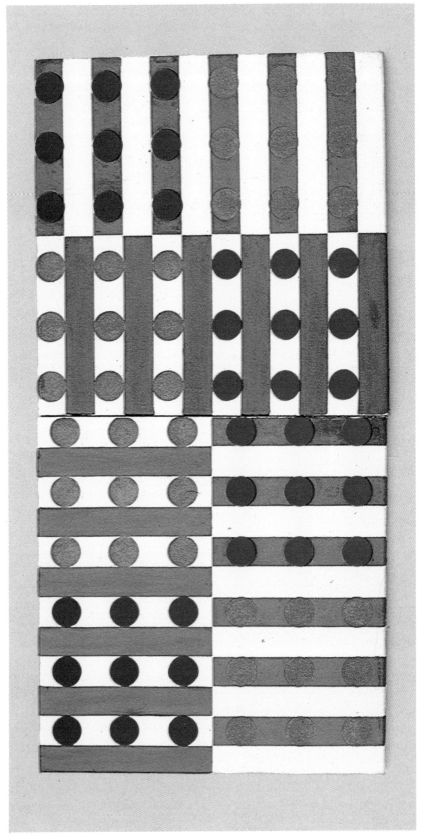

Left: Fig. 100 Shot silk showing 'atmospheric' effect of a blue warp when the fabric is angled so that it predominates. The 'fence' on the cliff top and the 'bush' on the hillside respectively show the pure colour and the slubbing characteristic of wild silk.

Fig. 99 These two butted identical paintings are made with one blue, one yellow, one red and one green. In painting these I was surprised to discover not that the reds and greens look different but that the difference is so much more marked when the ground is striped horizontally.

81

COLOUR CHART OF SYNONYMS

There may be some overlap of common usage of terms, but the following chart will show how confused the communication of colour can be:

TERM	THEORIST	PAINTER
colour	general term	general, or paint
hue	concerning wavelength emitted, transmitted or reflected. 'Family' whether it is orange or yellow: a yellowish hue	same
value	lightness/darkness as when photographed in black and white	same, or tone, or tonal value
high value	light	tints, diluted, low saturation, hue plus white or water
low value	dark	shades, hue plus black, low tone painting
chroma	intensity, strength of colour, saturation	same, plus brightness
high chroma	pure hue	bright, pure, high key
low chroma	impure hue (addition of grey, or complementary hue in dyes and pigments)	dull, tones of colour, low-key, muted
complementary colours	pairs of colours mixed to produce white (light) or black (neutral grey pigment, ink and dye)	same
neutral	a grey with no bias towards any colour	same
physical mix	paints or dyes mixed before application	same

'world'. A change of 'world' or patch causes the substitute patch or environment to appear coloured with the colour that is complementary to the first, e.g., the twilight sky appears to have changed to blue after you have been a few minutes in artificial yellow light.

Symbolic colour: red for hot taps, blue for cold, red for danger, green for safety.

Warm and cold colour: warm colours begin just in the blue-reds and go by yellow to finish in mid-green, cold colours are from mid-green through blue to red-purple. Warm and cold are relative. It is possible to have warm and cold yellow (marigold and lemon) and warm and cold blue (ultramarine and turquoise). In the context of particular objects, however, association and emotion can take over. Colour can create a warm or cold 'experience'. Take a yellow flame, for example, which is warm visually, intellectually, and as a tactile experience! Change to a blue flame – blue is a cold colour, but in this case the blue may be 'warm'.

TERM	DYER	FASHION/ COSMETICS
colour	general or dye-stuff★ or printing paste	general or overall effect of
hue	same. Wavelength particularly applicable where colour matching uses appropriate instruments	same (not the wavelength bit)
value	as painter	seldom used (confusion with monetary value?) tones instead
high value	pale shades or percent quoted	pale shades, light tones, pastels, candy colours
low value	deep or dark shades full strength dye, e.g., fully saturated purple	deep or dark shades or tones, rich (of purple and maroon)
chroma	as painter, saturation	seldom used
high chroma	saturated (bright colours)	bright, clear, clean
low chroma	flattened shades, toned or toned down	tones, muted, dull, muddy, neutrals, sombre, pastels, if high value, also neutrals
complementary	same	avoid confusion with complimentary
neutral	same	grey, beiges, sacking, natural and undyed, gold, silver, metallic
physical mix	non-homogeneous dye	not used

★ I.M.P. or Instrumental Match Prediction is made by measuring the red, green and blue components in a tri-stimulus colorimeter. This information with the colour characteristics of available dyes is computed and the dye recipe found. This is intended to speed up colour matching, taking out the skill and the tedium.

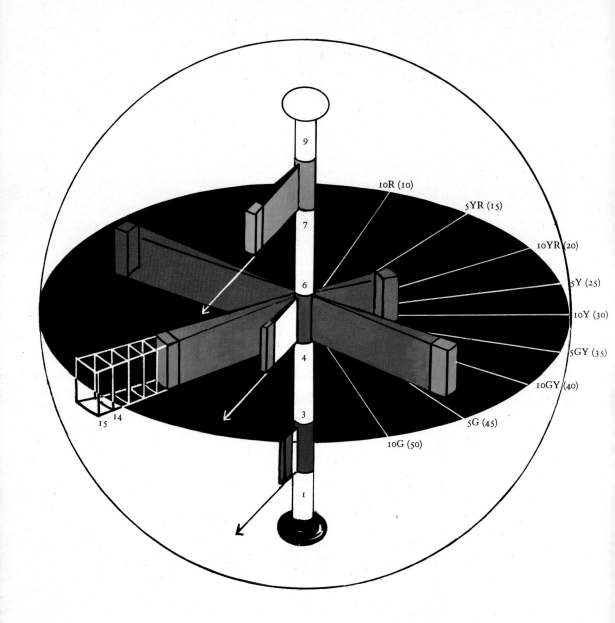

Labels on the figure (clockwise from upper right):

10R (10)
5YR (15)
10YR (20)
5Y (25)
10Y (30)
5GY (35)
10GY (40)
5G (45)
10G (50)

Numbers on the central column: 9, 7, 6, 4, 3, 1

Numbers near white skeleton: 15, 14

Fig. 102 The three components of colour: *hue* – the direction of the signpost fingers; *value* – high fingers are high value and light; *chroma* – tips of long fingers are brightest. Radial lines show main divisions for a ten-colour base (As Munsell). Each is sub-divided into ten parts. Alternative 1–100 system is shown in brackets. Parallel arrows show three values of the same blue-green hue. The white skeleton shows the positions for brighter blues than the one shown. The 'pink' (red-purple) can be estimated as brighter. The yellow opposite is considerably duller. The notation for the yellow may be written as 5Y 5/5 or 25-5/5 where 5Y = hue, 5 = value and /5 = chroma.

84

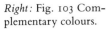

Right: Fig. 103 Complementary colours.

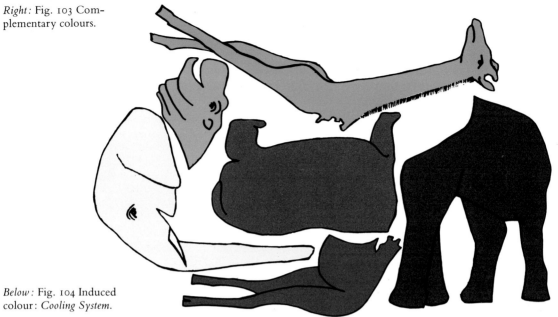

Below: Fig. 104 Induced colour: *Cooling System.*

Chapter 7
LIGHT

Fig. 105 Direct light at right angles shows the texture.

WITHOUT LIGHT YOU WOULDN'T SEE FABRICS. With subdued light you miss subtleties. With bright light everything is put on show. Direct light shining from near the viewer makes the textile appear at its shiniest. Direct light at right angles is like sunrise on cobbles and shows the texture of the fabric to full effect (Fig. 105). Direct light from behind a textile throws it into silhouette, like a sunset through a winter wood (Fig. 106).

   Most of our light is diffused. On planet Earth the atmosphere stops the sun shining harshly as a disc in a black sky. Even the shadow side is never wholly black. Under a cloudy sky diffusion is even greater (or conversely contrast is less). Much of European painting concerns itself with the beauty of gradual changes of light (Fig. 107). Fall-off of light

Fig. 106 Direct light from behind a textile throws it into silhouette, like sunset through a winter wood.

Fig. 107 The beauty of gradual changes of light: the increasing density of larch twigs.

in a room, so noticeable to photographers, was beautifully painted by Vermeer. There are long winter periods in northern regions where we view ourselves and our textiles more under artificial lighting than in daylight.

Some textiles are traditionally designed for use in the evening. So a designer should consider in what light or lights his fabric will be displayed to be sold and in which light or lights it will be used. There has been much romantic talk about the 'light' of St Ives, Paris or the Mediterranean since the Impressionists. Yet the lighting on their paintings in the galleries is inconstant or indifferent!

While the unity of the painting may overcome this and allow it to be seen favourably in a range of lights, I still feel that lighting is a highly underrated subject. Seeing a painting is an experience that may be dramatically influenced by its surroundings and lighting. In the short term both paintings and textiles in 'display' lighting may look attractive. In the long term both painting and fabric rely on their content.

The painting exists for itself. It is not a decoration but an object that yields more and more to the viewer as time goes by. The fabric in its life will have to withstand scrutiny in hard daylight, so it should be sold in store lighting which simulates hard daylight. The customer is then not disappointed and likely to return for more.

Equally, discotheque clothes should be sold in disco lighting, even though they appear crude in the summer sun outside the boutique door. For example, as mentioned in Chapter 6, a brown fabric from a brown dye may appear brown in artificial light, while in the street it may appear reddish in hue. Another garment which matched it indoors stays the same. The first garment, although brown, may be made from a dye composed of reds and greens. Like so many aspects of textiles someone will one day make a life's work of studying the effects of this strange phenomenon which can be given the name of 'metameric colour'.

My main concern, however, is to draw attention to the beauty that is reflected by the delicate arrangement of mirrors that we see as everyday textiles. Understanding exactly why they are beautiful is only useful if, while designing textiles, you know when to apply the knowledge.

There is a whole fascinating world of light involved when using special effects. What illusions of light and colour can be created on stage are best left to a stage magician to explain. It is quite enough to appreciate that the light is reflected from or passed through every textile that you see in ordinary daylight, such as Britain on a cloudy day. It is light and our past knowledge that tell us why nylon and cotton look different. It begins with the molecules.

If you put a stick into water it appears to bend at the surface, the point where air and water meet. It is the light that bends of course, not the stick, and the same thing happens with the long chain molecule of a textile. But light entering the end of the molecule bends at a different angle. (If you could tip water on its side and put in the stick, it would appear bent at a different angle.) Each fibre type has two different angles. This is the first stage in causing the visible difference in appearance. If the molecule chains are stretched and made more parallel, they reflect more light in one area. Put another way, the mirrors are arranged in orderly rows and face the same way, making a large collective mirror. Try stretching a piece of chewing gum or rubber and see the effect take place before your eyes.

This parallelization and reflectivity goes on up through fibres and yarns. The easiest to imagine are strip filament yarns. These yarns are ripped from sheets or made by extending a fluid through dumb-bell section slots in a spinneret. The mirrors are comparatively large and the areas switch suddenly from dark to light as the fibre twists.

When a fibre is triangular in section this suggests that one part in three will, in the same position, reflect as one in two before. Silk is roughly – and 'roughly' is the key to the aesthetic success of natural fibres – triangular in section, accounting for the fine sparkle. Fibres can be more subdivided until they are striated with grooves which form many more smaller mirrors. Viscose rayon has this character (see Chapter 3).

When the mirror is rounded, or the fibre is made of 'lobes', then the mirror is graduated and moves across the fibre with you as your eyes move. The more pure the cylinder, then the more mechanical the fibre looks. Efforts are usually made to lose this in the spinning by fancy spinning (gimp effects) or in the weaving by fancy weaving (crêpe weaves). Cuprammonium rayon, nylon, and other synthetics have circular cross-sections. Acetate is striated like viscose but rounded, which partly accounts for its soft appearance. Silk also falls into this category and trilobal nylon sets out to change the blandness of standard nylon.

Fibres which in their standard form are bright, may be dulled by a delustring agent like titanium dioxide, which is added to the spinning fluid.

It is no wonder that cotton normally has a matt look. Under a microscope the fibres look worse than badly treated drinking straws. Their faces are broken and irregular and the skin shrivelled. Pumping them full of caustic soda and stretching them tightly causes the cylinders to fill out and the wrinkles to disappear, making a softly shining yarn characteristic of mercerization.

We can follow the yarn through into a type of weaving dependent on light for its effect: damask, which is usually all white or self colour. Collective mirrors are made by packing threads into a satin-sateen structure. The threads lie so that they come to the surface seven times out of eight – a satin structure. At right angles to this the same thing is happening to form a sateen structure.

I have jumped from fibre to yarn to structure. Obviously once one has grasped the idea of parallelizing to make collective mirrors, then it is easy to see that continuous filament yarns are likely to be much brighter than yarns spun from fibres. Straight yarns in a woven structure will make brighter areas than looped yarns in knitting. The twist of yarns can be used effectively too, though this is very subtle – a pattern may be formed by having a block of 'S' twist yarns followed by a block of 'Z' twist yarns. Perhaps you have looked at the silver and gold foil tiles that are to be found in home-decorating shops – they rely on just this principle.

Lustrous yarns are impossible to match for colour – at least for tonal value – unless the sample and match threads are orientated in the

same way. With carpet yarns it is the *ends* of the tufts that you are concerned with. The richness of strong colour in any pile fabric, whether carpet or velvet, is due to the absorption of light in its depth.

Lighted white areas appear to take up more space than they actually occupy. A four-foot satellite can still be seen though it is miles above us. Thousands of white areas where threads cross in a net curtain means that anyone spying from a sunny street would be dazzled by the reflectivity of the surface (Fig. 108). Looking out from the comparatively dark room is like looking through a thin web. You need very little information from the scene outside to know what is going on. At night the position of the bright light is reversed. This gauze effect, well used for stage back-drops, becomes a handy vehicle for decorative effects in textiles. It becomes particularly fascinating to mix surface-reflecting yarns with open structures such as leno and lace (Fig. 109). Silhouettes may be made on such open structures by printing with flock or burning out (see Chapter 8 and Fig. 110). These densely patterned areas in turn cast shadows perhaps in a new shape of ephemeral beauty (Fig. 111).

Dull or uninteresting fabrics are often relieved or highlit by using shiny or metallic yarns singly or in groups – the cheapest shiny rayon dyed a pale dull yellow can look like real gold metal. The secret, if there is one, about light used in textiles is to use the brightest part in the smallest quantities. This rule, applied to colour too, is very safe, and it is to be preferred to an arbitrariness and lack of meaning in positioning and amount.

Fig. 108 Anyone spying from a sunny street is dazzled by the reflectivity of the surface. Looking out from a comparatively dark room is like looking through a thin web.

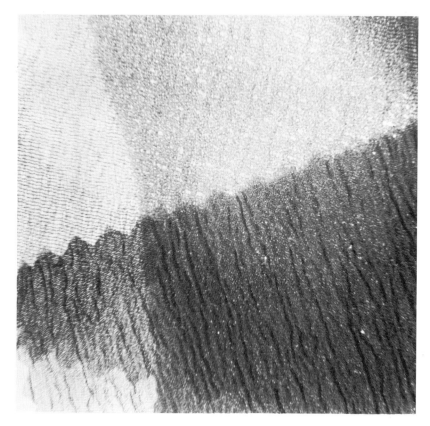

Fig. 109 Mixing surface-reflecting yarns: crêpon and metallized gauze.

Fig. 110 It is difficult to see which is real or transient, which is silhouette or shadow, in this flock print.

Fig. 111 Patterned areas cast shadows, perhaps in a new shape of ephemeral beauty.

Chapter 8
ON THE SURFACE

A TEXTILE IS A SKIN with an inside and an outside, a face and a back (Fig. 113). You can never see it totally sculpturally, as you might a chair or a table, because you are dependent on what the dress designer or interior designer does. You can make a stiff or floppy fabric, which gives them clues as to how to use it. If you print it with a jazzy pattern, then the designer would waste his time using fancy seams Fig. 112. But even though you can inhibit the shape, you are for the greater part more like a painter than a sculptor. You can print on flat areas and be a bas-relief expert when it comes to dealing with the minute rough surfaces of structural textiles.

What do you think about when you think of textile design? What do you think about when you think of art? Most people you ask will see coloured shapes decorating a piece of cotton, a printed textile. Art to them is a taut canvas and a stabbing paint brush, a painting. People go straight to the product which epitomizes the subject. If you take the cotton for printing, or the canvas for painting, you narrow the subjects to purely technical processes. So what else is there? Well, the cotton and canvas can be seen as 'supports'. Plainly these supports will hold any mark it is possible to make. What do you need to make a mark? Paint or ink and an appliance. Is this enough? No, the work still needs shape. Shape needs an idea – even the idea to make 'non-form'. Textile or art both need an *idea*.

The quality of the idea must be the highest possible. There is no question about one design being better than another in abstract. As soon as commerce is brought in, the quality of an idea becomes determined by how effective it is on those who are meant to receive it.

A 'good' design to designers may embody subtleties which would cause the man-in-the-street to dislike it. It would, therefore, be a 'bad' design if you were intending to sell to the mass market.

It would be easy to criticize an idea on television as being childish, implying low quality; however, the same idea in a children's show might seem appropriate. Kids need the security of the good guy winning in the end. Grown-ups perhaps need either a twist in the plot or a different idea altogether. Grown-ups might enjoy a bit of good photography. This would perhaps embroider a lower quality artistic idea. The idea of the producer may be that good photography on a thin inartistic idea would give him the biggest audience. And therefore the quality of *his* idea as a producer was good.

The world's leading artist may have an audience of none because

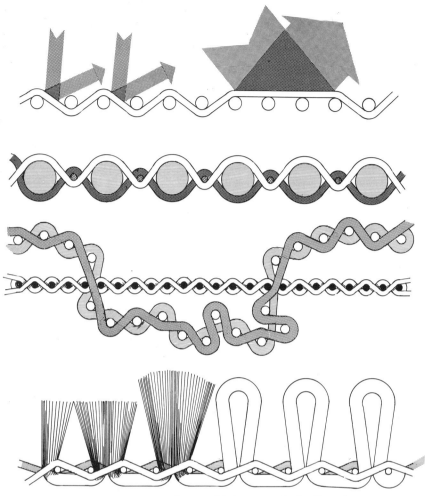

Fig. 112 These four cross-sections of woven fabrics are not basic. They show, however, some of the important design characteristics.

First: one thread in plain weave turning into 'float' as might occur in 5-end satin or 4 and 1 twill. Tone shows how light reflected to the eye is broken or continuous.

Second: shows light and dark threads are crossed with thick (light) and thin (dark) threads. The dominant light thread could be decorative and weak, and the structure strengthened by the thin thread.

Third: shows two interwoven plain fabrics. Although woven flat, probably one thread face, one thread back alternately, the fabric may be shrunk afterwards. The thin fabric, sometimes on the face and sometimes underneath, contracts. The remainder has to go somewhere . . . Several principles are embodied here. The cockling fabric could be instead a single thread – the face and back cloths could be even – 'solid' colour areas are possible.

The fourth section shows cropped pile (velvet); cut but uncropped pile (corduroy) is similar; uncut pile (towelling) is left in this state. Tufted carpets are not unlike this, though the pile thread is *punched* through a backing to predetermined heights and left looped, cut or cropped as in the diagram. Other carpets are more complicated, but are usually loop or pile.

his ideas are ahead of his time (he could, of course, be working success-fully commercially at a lower level in the same pieces of work). Let us leave *idea* for a moment.

When Marcel Duchamp displayed his urinal back in 1917, he at once questioned the need for craftsmanship and at the same time jolted the viewer into comment. There was hardly a better way of showing

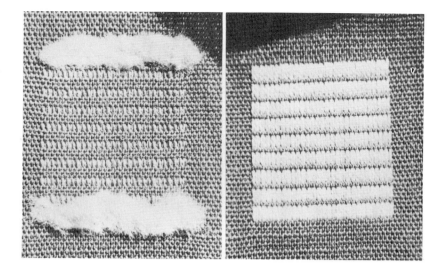

Fig. 113 A textile is a skin with an inside and an outside, a face and a back. Here 'extra' warp is woven-in and clipped. Either the 'fuzz' may be regarded as the feature or the 'clean' square which is on the alternative side.

the people who saw it (and by proxy me) that a work of art needs a beholder. A dialogue, as artists say, is set up between the work and the viewer. The more you give in looking and thinking, the more you get back as a reward. The better the painting – and it doesn't have to have shock tactics – the greater the experience. So we have *experience*.

It's but a short step to subtract the artifact and just tell you what to experience. We now have a 'happening' and 'walk-round' sculpture. For example, I could tell you to walk clockwise round the old Grammar School at Market Harborough at noon on a September day looking up at about seven feet from the ground (Fig. 114). I would have more control over your experience than John Constable would have if you went to the National Gallery and stared for the same length of time at *The Hay Wain*. I have at least as much effect on you as if I had made this edifice myself – at least as far as the physical process of looking is concerned – and all for free! Another word has emerged: *process*.

Technique can be done badly or well and is therefore allied to skill. Process is the method of operation, and artists are currently examining process. Art has gradually forsaken any one technique. Now the equivalent of a composer's music is written and exhibited on the gallery wall, telling you to play it. It is, in fact, interesting to compare 'art' with the other arts. Composers, for example, have been using abstract sounds since music began. In fact figurative forms (bird-calls) or secondhand forms (familiar tunes) are rare. The decision to invert notes is intellectual – a process. And if B, A, C, H, justify the basis for melody, why not use the colours orange, yellow, red and purple as variations for the artist. The pianist must be a technician, however virtuoso and highly skilled an interpreter.

The Dynamic Square (Fig. 115, see p. 104) provides a way of creating variations with colour. It has 30 × 30 squares and the instructions are as follows. . . .

Initially regard as paired vertically (30 divisions across and 15 up). From bottom left paint no. 15 green – also its upper partner. Step by pairs up and left to finish top left. Call this 'track HCG' (H = halfway along side, C = corner, G = Green) (Track 1). Rotate work 90° left, paint track CHR (bottom left vertical pairs of right-hand steps up to

93

halfway of new top line) (Track 2). The first upper square will already be green. Accept this and adopt a principle of 'first come, first served' throughout. Rotate 180°. Begin Track HCB as track HCG (3). Rotate 90° left, paint track CHR (4); 180° left, HCB (5); 90° left CHG (6); 180° left HCR (7); 90° left CBB (8); and 180° to starting point (9).

Repeat complete circuit as many times as necessary to fill area using the following principle: use an inner and outer area for each unit. The outer area stays constant for nine tracks. The inner area is the same as the base colour track that it follows.

2nd circuit is right of first, blue around track colour.

3rd circuit is left of first, red around track colour.

4th circuit is right of 2nd circuit, green around track colour.

5th circuit is left of third, blue around track colour.

6th circuit is right of fourth, red around track colour.

7th circuit is left of fifth, green around track colour.

8th circuit is right of 6th, blue around track colour and so on to completion.

Actors are highly skilled resurrectionists who revive from time to time the sounds of Shakespeare which lie entombed in black print. The playwright's process is to record words and rudimentary stage directions and to allow interpretation. The film-maker snaps and snips and re-arranges time as never before. The photographer places familiar objects in any unlikely place – opening his shutters on to surrealism. Photography, because of its proliferation of 'formula' snaps and 'how-to-do-it' approaches, has helped us to realize that it is the seeing and not the holding of the pencil that is important (Fig. 116). It irons out the technical difficulties of making a realistic picture. Technology is doing our slogging craftsmanship for us. But do our ideas match up to it?

All this may seem a long way to go to get back to our piece of cotton or our canvas taut on its stretcher. I'd like nothing better than to flood them with great masses of colour, but I am not talking to

Fig. 114 The old Grammar School at Market Harborough, Northamptonshire.

Fig. 116 Photography has helped us to realise that it is the 'seeing' that is important.

94

Above right: Fig. 117
Cloqué: the fine threads
contract, causing the
other areas to cockle.
The areas are reversed
on the back. See cross-
section diagram too.

Sunday artists now – or to pleasure-seekers. Often the *idea* makes this
nice therapeutic gesture superfluous.

What is the least we need to do to get across the idea? A freshly
washed cotton shirt looks like rag. Yet after the press of a smoothing-
iron it is gently shining and beautifully draping – a type of transformation
more significantly acceptable than a shirt also freshly washed but then
with a design printed on it (all other things being equal). This, of course,
is only hypothetical. The modification of a surface may be an afterthought and progressive, or it can be part of a calculated process in both
art and textiles. I will now mention some textile modifications and later
show how similar they are to art processes.

In textiles most surfaces may be modified physically or chemically.
The process of manufacture may, and in fact usually does, take into
account the fact that further modifications will be made. Fabrics
which come flat off a machine may undergo wet or dry heat and may
be made to pucker in a controlled way. This is vital to the appearance
of such fabrics as cloqués and blister effects (Fig. 117). Other fabrics
may be sold with a simple calender finish. The same fabric with frequent
but minor faults may be sent off to be printed (afterthought). Usually
fabrics are constructed with printing in mind (planning). These can be
made more cheaply than would be acceptable for plain fabrics.

A finisher, like most other processors in the line, looks at the work
which comes to him just as raw material until he has handled it. He
does in fact handle most fabrics, though some colour woven fabrics
come straight off the loom and will just be inspected and packed. At
the other extreme of usage there are canvases and webbings which may
be sold unfinished. In between these the majority of fabrics are rather
sad in the loom or 'grey' state, and will only come to life in the finishing
department. Going round a factory can be very boring if you are expect-
ing to see colourful designs.

Woollen fabrics are traditionally woven a little 'open' and then

95

beaten with sticks and stones and washed. The fibres separate out, the fabric shrinks a little, takes on a 'lofty' appearance and has a warmer, softer handle. The next stage could be to raise up a fluffy surface by brushing with teasles. This surface is then 'sheared' (lightly trimmed) or 'cropped' (a heavier cut). These processes are still being done by hand as well as by machine.

But whether by sticks, stones and teasles, or by fallers for beating and steel wires for teasling, the effect is startling. Colours become intimately mixed and the fabrics become smoother or softer to touch. The construction is often lost under the overall surface, such as you find in flannel or blankets. Colours in fibre mixtures are closer to pigment mixes. Ultramarine blue and lemon yellow, for example, look grey when seen together in optical mixtures as stitches, but will turn green when brushed. Pattern designers and colourists must take this finishing process into account.

There are many subtleties in textile finishing, but local names serve to make the subject more difficult than it should be. Making a fluffy surface, for example, can be called napping, genapping, or gigging. Less esoterically this process may also be called raising, brushing or teasling. 'Gassing' cotton, sometimes in the yarn, sometimes in the fabric, is a form of smoothing by getting rid of unwanted hairs. The fabric or yarn passes rapidly through burning gas-jets. Cotton is similar to other cellulose fibres such as linen and those reconstituted by man – viscose rayon, secondary and tertiary cellulose acetate (recognizable in such trade-names as 'rayon', those having 'av' or 'cela' in the name, and dicel, tricel, and arnel). Characteristically their recovery is bad   in other words, they crease badly, except for tricel which is heat-set for life. They are good candidates for heat and pressure like the calender process, the industrial equivalent of the domestic smoothing iron, where the fabric passes between heavy metal rollers, one or more of which are usually heated. If you are passing a fabric through heated metal rolls of a friction calender, you speed up one roller. The resultant skidding causes a glazed effect. (Engraving a roller with a pattern will result in a relief pattern showing on an 'embossed' fabric.) A more subtle effect, which relies on 'interference' patterns, is when a ribbed fabric passes ever-so-slightly out of true under a roller which is engraved with 'ribs' similar to those in the fabric. A pattern is formed which, with all the characteristics of natural patterning, is always roughly the same but never actually repeats itself. This in fact looks water-like and takes the French word 'moiré' (Fig. 118). Many of these processes, applied to cellulose fibres, are more or less impermanent.

Chemical impregnations often increase both appearance, handle and serviceability. Staple rayon or 'spun', as it is sometimes called, can be given a new and almost permanent body. Fabrics can be lacquered or used as a base for plastic coating. In wallcoverings and in tufted carpets the stability of the product is totally dependent on its backing, which is applied liquid and allowed to set. There are other integral processes in textiles – the bonding of fibres or the bonding of fabrics – which are not really the subject of a chapter dealing with the modification of surfaces.

There are numerous applications of chemicals which can be added to make fabrics retardant, resistant, repellent or proof against all the usual hazards which don't actually constitute wearing out. These, of

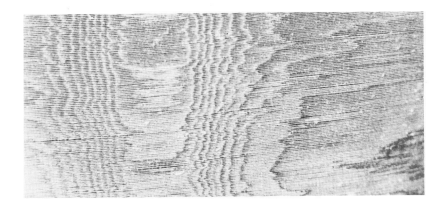

Fig. 118 Moiré water effect interference pattern.

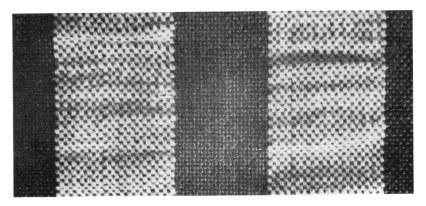

Fig. 119 Seer-sucker: the light band was fed in on the loom with heavier weights than the dark band. It now tries to recover – a typical structural textile process where the effect is planned ahead.

course, are such everyday threats as water, dirt, stains, and fire-causing cigarette ends. Wrinkles and creasing I have mentioned, but how about filling up silk with salts of tin to make it weigh heavier and drape better? Plissé effects make a cheap, impermanent 'seersucker' – a cockling of cellulose fibres by adding caustic soda (Fig. 119). Sulphuric acid, however, destroys cotton, and if a fabric is made by blending fibres of cotton with fibres of an acid-resistant fibre such as a polyester (terylene/dacron), then areas of fabric may be thinned away.

A polyester cotton lawn already possessing pleasant properties of surface appearance, drape, easy wash and anti-crease is made even more seductive by having areas printed to an even greater degree of translucency. The cotton fibres are devoured by the acid, giving an easy-to-remember name for the process – 'dévoré'.

Bleaching is a chemical modification, and stentering a physical modification. Stentering is straightening the yarns and setting the fabric to a desired width. These processes often precede printing. This makes for happier customers when they find that their patterns and the 'grain' of the cloth match up.

Dyeing, too, is a form of modification, but it is usually treated as a separate subject. Dyeing as an after-process of fabrics or in the 'piece' is seldom so attractive as when the yarn is dyed before manufacture, and a colour is made of two hues. This was mentioned previously in dealing with colour. Cross-dyed effects with different yarns or dye-variant yarns can make beautiful effects which are often not fully exploited.

Decatizing or the setting of woollens and worsteds to a stable position has been taken further with man's synthetics. Here the fabric

97

or garment may have creases set in it at temperatures above those likely to be encountered in washing, and of course below those temperatures at which the fibres melt, producing trousers and skirts with creases for life. This process of setting thermoplastic yarns is not to be confused with 'thermo-set' plastics, which are plastics made to set once only. Further heating only serves to degrade them.

Mercerizing, still one of the most important discoveries in textiles, was the one in which cotton fabric was immersed in caustic soda and used nearly a third less dye for the same shade than before. Alternatively colours could be stronger. More than that, John Mercer discovered in 1844 that when yarn was stretched while immersed, it became brighter and increased up to nearly a third more in strength.

Now let us move away from the area where a process is all effective to the more familiar ones where the process is of less importance, and the techniques and 'design' are more obvious. But cringe with me when you hear someone say they are going to 'put a bit more design' into something. Design grows out of manufacture by necessity. Much of what follows is about the 'inessential' or decorative element that is added to sell a fabric. As with the finisher, up to this point all the skill put in to structuring a textile has only yielded a raw material for the printer.

For artists who are familiar with the processes of lino, woodcut, etching and screen print, it is salutary in passing to compare these processes with textiles. Lino and woodcuts are primarily relief prints. The ink on the surface of the block is transferred to the fabric. These can be done by the student by using lino but adding flock. Flock, short lengths of cotton or rayon fibre almost like a dust, is glued on to cut lino. This holds more printing paste than base lino.

A little professional block printing is still carried on. Blocks of pear or holly wood studded with copper pins are inked and struck home into the fabric with the aid of a mallet. The equivalent of etching in textiles is the roller print. Here copper rolls are varnished and the designs are cut through the varnish. Dipping in acid causes the line to be etched into the copper to the required depth. In printing the engraved copper roll is coated with printing paste and cleaned by the 'doctor' blade. The paste left in the grooves is sucked out by the fabric passing by under pressure. As with intaglio etching the lines present no problem, but solid areas need to have a repetition of plateaux to support the fabric throughout and valleys to hold the fluid. The rollers are cut with grooves. In etching the effect can be made by granules (Fig. 120).

With screen printing, a medium which is ever improving in both the art and textile field, it is easier to point out the differences as there

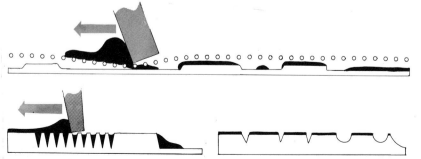

Fig. 120 Cross-section of screen print showing squeegee pushing paste or ink through screen mesh ('O's) on to a rough surface (see also Fig. 81). Surface being cleaned ready for intaglio printing, etching, roller printing of textiles. Surface inked for relief print (wood-engraving and woodcut).

98

are so many similarities. With the slight exception of pigments, which are applied to the surface of textiles and subsequently baked, all textile printing is transparent. Another difference is that the screen and its 'jig-saw' pattern area is moved along the fabric, usually on alternate repeats to avoid 'marking off' from the bottom of the screen. Printing on paper is done item-wise by hinging or lifting the screen and taking the paper to the printing table.

The two methods are brought closer together when in the machine screen printing of textiles the fabric is moved by a conveyor belt under the screens. Also in the process of sublistatic printing a pre-printed paper transfer may be transferred from the paper to a garment by a heated press.

The more recent space-saving versions of screen printing use rotary screens. The 'silk' screen, which is usually polyester/polyamide mesh in modern textiles, is changed now to a delicately perforated phosphor-bronze cylinder. The printing paste is fed inside and the screen moves round the squeegee to force out the coloured paste. As with traditional textile printing, the pattern has been previously formed by blanking off from the light the area that is to be printed. This is done with a full size hand-painted film (negative) placed over the screen, which has been coated in low light with a light sensitive emulsion and allowed to dry. When the negative is in position the bright light is switched on. After a few minutes the screen is washed and the areas that have been shaded have not been fixed by the action of the light and will get washed away. They form the printed pattern areas.

Whereas printing on paper is complete, the process on textiles is usually incomplete until the printed areas or local dyebaths have been fixed into the fabric. This is done by taking the fabric into a steamer. The curing of pigment printing onto the fabric is done by dry heat.

One printing process can produce results much like another, but there are subtleties which distinguish one technique from another. Hand screen prints, for example, are marginally richer in colour than machine screen prints which, in turn, are slightly more desirable than roller printed. There are give-away characteristics, visible to experts, associated with roller and screen processes. There is often a line roller which makes the even 'stylo' outline of flowers on a cotton print, a mechanical translation of the artist's black pen line. The other characteristic artist's flaw of an uneven wash is interpreted by two rollers. One is a 'wash' roller for a tint of the hue, which is flat, while the second roller is used for 'modelling' with a similar but darker hue. One side of an area is cut to hold more dye and gradually tapered off to print nothing on the other. All this because an artist can't lay a flat wash!

Flat washes tightly fitted, i.e. with colour A butting or appearing to butt against colour B, are a characteristic of artist-printers using optical effects on paper. Turquoise on orange, for example, is easy, because the turquoise is opaque and covers the orange. In textiles any form of overlap here would make a muddy brown.

A possible solution is to 'discharge' print. Here a piece of fabric is dyed in one of the colours and then printed with a chemical which strips off the colour in the required pattern. But added to this stripper is the second type of dye colour which is helped on by the chemical that strips off the first one. The orange and turquoise may be a little dull, however, as not all dyes match paints, and a dye for this method might be of a dull class.

It is, of course, possible to go on deeper than the purpose of this book. You can either have deep technological knowledge and possibly be restricted by what you think you can't do, or be an artist and allow for interpretation. If the artist is way-off the possibilities, then the work will not be worth doing; if the technologist is insensitive, then a subtle shape or colour will be mechanized or rationalized in a detrimental way and the point will be lost.

A totally different area for comparison in art forms and textiles is the use of light as the medium and the textile as a modifier. Although dévoré printing as previously mentioned functions in this way, the emphasis here is on the fabric. If you make a net curtain and superimpose thickened areas, it is then possible to see this as a textile, as suspended silhouettes, as a pierced shade, or you may look from this to the shadows it casts.

In flock printing gum is applied to the net, usually by a screen printing method, and short flock fibres are applied, usually electrostatically. There is no equivalent art form, although photograms and simple figure and ground work in any art form immediately involve similar problems. There is an inherent coarseness which makes flock on net a difficult medium of doing what it was intended to do – make a cheap substitute for lace. And like Persian rugs translated on to cheap Axminster, they look like cheap copies. We are undoubtedly conditioned by what we know.

Maybe it is partly sentiment which makes us feel the directness of a woodcut or an etching by an old master. The choice of woodcut is closely allied either to what the artist is trying to say about forms being related simply to their own background or to what he is being forced to say by the limitations of the technique.

With etching, space and volume is etched, line by line, until the form gradually emerges. In screen printing on textiles the feeling of woodcut or etching could be interpreted by a skilful designer, but this would only emerge as a style and not as vital to the work. If an effect is gained which is not vital to a work, then the work suffers by its lack of vitality. Vitality is often mistaken for boldness, but fine sensitive work can be vital too. It needs a trained eye to distinguish between vital and slack work, because both could be 'realistically' like the objects they were drawn from. And before making a judgement you must know a little of what the artist was trying to do. Only then can you test the work for irrelevancies. Then each part should be interdependent, either visually or intellectually, on the others in the composition.

In this chapter, more so than in the others, I have tried to show that even when the design process is already largely done, some vital modification may be necessary in the finishing of the fabric. This modification may be worth more than any design put on a surface – it depends on the idea. I have also tried comparing art with textiles, and to help understand this it is assumed that you already knew a little about the art-making processes.

Chapter 9
MORE THOUGHTS

Now is the time for summing up. I want to make sure that I have made my point that textiles are not easy or superficial, yet not too frighteningly scientific or technical. If I have frightened off a few who are afraid of hard work, then I hope I have gained a few brainy young men who may have thought this a cissy job. I also hope I may have shown a few would-be pure artists that there is an untapped potential in textiles and maybe an alternative career.

For much of the detail in Chapter 3 I am indebted to R. W. Moncrieff and his book *Man-Made Fibres*. Here I have attempted to show that there are so many points where details could be altered. Each tiniest alteration is reduplicated so that the overall result is vastly affected.

Somewhere you may have drawn the conclusion that designing is largely a team job and that the job isn't complete until the customer is satisfied and perhaps returns for more. Michael Farr in *Design Management* (London 1966) shows how you walk a knife edge of success and failure. You are only part of a chain, and although some links are more humble than yours, they manifest themselves as people with highly specialized skills. On occasions they can offer you the answer to a problem of your own speciality if you are big enough to take it.

In Chapters 4 and 5 I failed to mention how form could be arranged by systems such as the golden mean, the golden section and the Fibonacci series. These are well covered elsewhere and are not wholly relevant. At least form in textiles has been shown to be seldom flat or graphic, even in prints where the surface is folded.

I have perhaps disclosed a trade secret or two which will be readily used by the 'systems' artist. The words on random and chance, too, should be compared to the writing and music of John Cage.

Colour should emphatically be taken for what I have said rather than for what I have illustrated. The best colour scheme defies analysis and though it makes a book more attractive it would serve only to illustrate itself. I hope I have shown that colour just does not do that. It must have a *context*.

I have shown how light relates to the microcosmic aspects of textiles. Refraction, reflections and shadows should never be forgotten as a source of pattern either. A couple of bits of coloured paper and some reflecting surfaces, or a light and some grids, and you should never be short of a motif.

Lastly I have shown that surfaces are often 'latent' – part of a predetermined process as well as the well-known support for printing.

I am not sure whether it was a compliment or not when a colleague said, 'Only you would show students examples of bad work!' I was hoping when I began this book that it would be picked up casually because it was visually attractive, cause someone to flick through it and then find themselves hours later in an uncomfortable position with the library or bookshop lights going out around them. The next day they would join our world of textiles for life. I thought I would make every page a carefully laid out picture with diagrams so clear as to make captions superfluous, and with illustrations of only beautiful objects.

Then I found how imperfect a medium the book is. Mistakes and bad work should either be made by the student and corrected or shown to him. In the book I need to explain points, and this cannot always be done with beautiful visuals. Our approach to a book is just like the one to textiles that goes 'Oh I don't like the look of that'. We judge so many things on first sight by what *we* like. It would have been easy to have collected a few exquisitely coloured illustrations that would have made a rapport between me and a particular body of people. These would only have served to prolong the arrogance of artists who, because it is their life, find a different set of values from non-specialists. The artist can live in his cloud and draw reference from the everyday world when he wishes. The designer must live on the ground but can jump as high as he needs to do for his own soul.

As I said at the beginning and several times since, I am trying to redress the balance as I find it. Because of this the book does not set out to give a balanced picture of the priorities for successful designing. I am sure that it is not the purpose of a college to do this either. College will probably always be the place where wilder experiments are carried out. Bringing home the realism of delivering the goods on time and repeating orders – often very difficult things for an experimental artist – is only a minor responsibility of a college.

However I don't agree with letting students do only as they fancy and showing them *only* 'good' or 'classy' examples. This perpetuates the breed. You get some flattering results in terms of immediate work and everyone kids everyone else and themselves that things are going well, but the design, like the breed, goes a little weak in the head.

The head contains most of the equipment that should be exercised by a designer. The eyes and the brain are the equipment of the age of technology. The hand presses the button. The best graphic artists may need to handle a camera for sheer speed, but being able to draw will always be a vital skill that can be turned to profit as well as to Sunday enjoyment.

If any hand-weavers have been discouraged by my playing down the therapeutic arts, then don't be. In an age when technology reigns supreme there is automatically an inbuilt reaction to it. You can therefore make money or at least keep alive by doing your thing on a hand-loom. But please *try* to do something new. The world will soon be crying out for real craftsmanship. Much of the peasant art that we see is their interpretation of what they think we want. As comedian Tom Lehrer puts it, the only thing wrong with folk music is that it is written by the people. We used to have motifs that came from the East and travelled slowly across the medieval continent, being tolerably refined by the medieval pace. Nowadays technology gives us instant rubbish

Fig. 121 The camera is
the pattern seeker's
notebook.

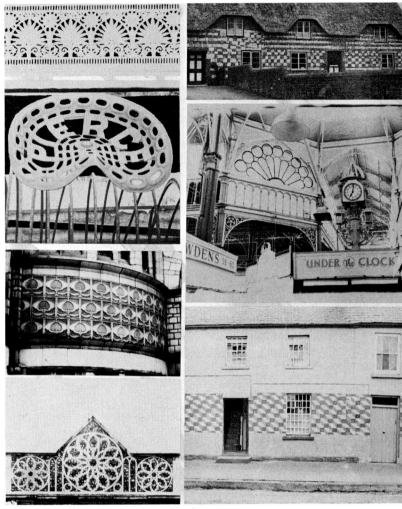

which flies east, is copied and flies west again in days.

I would be a defeatist to spend time urging a return to an earlier and perhaps more real civilization such as the Greeks had. I have few romantic urges to live in a past age. (Have you noticed that people never see themselves as the slaves?) We are born in a technological age, so let's get the best out of it. If you love beautiful things get a top job and fill our world with beautiful objects.

The head, as I said a little while ago, contains our tools. The hand presses the button. I urge you to read Edward de Bono on thinking, although what he says would put me out of work as a teacher for most of the time. He says that thinking can be taught as a thing in itself, not as a by-product of a conventional education learning something else. I had come to a parallel conclusion before discovering him. This is based on the idea that understanding a subject can often be made better by involving oneself in exercises that are slightly removed from it (no high jumper will spend all his time leaping).

This I know is not quite the same, but it is probably a reaction against the how-to-do-it approach, where a student is not encouraged to find his own answers. I must just add here that my childhood teachers were just such books, so that I owe much of my initial stimulation to

103

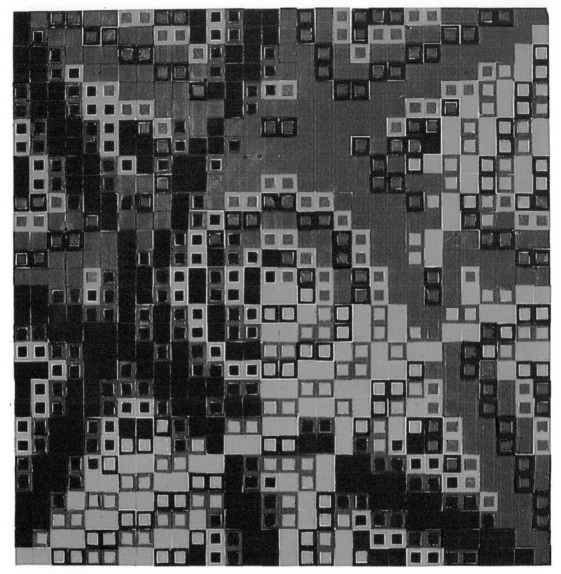

Fig. 115 The Dynamic
Square.

them. However we are living in an age when culture is fast becoming
universalized by radio, TV, Sunday colour supplements and international fashion. It is therefore inevitable that we must seek to break our
patterns of thought to provide originality in design. I often encourage
students to have an education in one subject and get a career in another
if they can. Mixing breeds usually strengthens; a fashion student will
press weavers to use fashionable yarns and colours and a weaving specialist
will know how to provide the fabric for the dress designing.

Creativity is a complicated process. Designing that has any degree
of originality is usually either the result of a great deal of hard physical
slog or mental activity *plus* an indefinable something, romantically and
popularly known as inspiration. How many people have said that successful work is 99 per cent perspiration and one per cent inspiration? In
Chapter 9 with most of the illustrations completed I can endorse the bit
about perspiration. Even allowing for redressing any balance, I must
reiterate this platitude. There is no short cut, even for naturals. I am not

a great biography reader, but it seems that most successful people have had to struggle for long periods.

Creativity, and I have seen it happen many times, needs to be there in you, and it must be continually exercised like a sprinter's legs in winter. For the odd, and unfortunately often short, amount of time you are called on to use it, it mustn't fail you. Creativity cannot be taught – even de Bono would admit this – but apart from climbing into rarified air, there is little danger, and almost everything to be gained, from looking and thinking constantly, and in as many different ways as possible.

Much of structural textiles is dependent on careful planning and choosing, necessitating logic, so it is easy to fall into the trap of thinking that the logical answer is right. Logic, along with tidiness and rationalization, may have little to do with creativity. The creative urge must override technical difficulties, laziness, and deadlines – and this is not easy.

With textiles even more than with other media, it is very difficult to produce anything really new. New yarns, like new type faces in books, make textiles appear different, but the structures are much the same as ever.

A large amount of commercial success depends on producing the goods at the right time. As I have mentioned before, timing has to be right. All that can be learned in college, and more, has to be used as second nature. You need to work within the structure of your market. The great cartoonist Ffeiffer drew a succession of pictures showing a writer having high falutin' ideas and finally finishing with a statement which said that the hallmark of the good professional is a profound knowledge of his market. If your market is dependent on close timing, as with fashion-orientated textiles, then you must see that this is fulfilled. If your market is more dependent on your personal skills, you must maintain those.

This leads me to remind you again that you are not a designer to please yourself but that you are offering a service. To the customer you are not a designer but a source. When the item you have offered is worn out, the customer may return for a repeat or a similar item. The artist or designer must decide whether or not to repeat that item or, as he

Left and right : Fig. 122 The weather and a change of light can suggest new relationships. Art and design often rely on the ability to see significance in juxtapositioning simple, ordinary things.

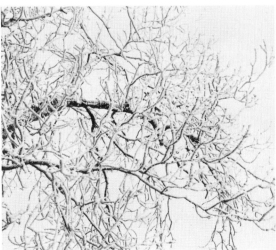

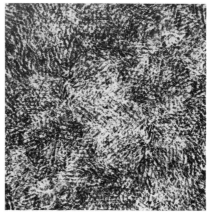

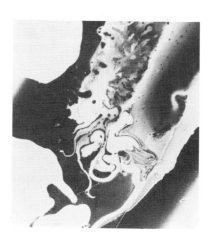

Left: Fig. 123 In the same way that Monet built himself a water-lily pool to help him paint his landscapes of light, you can invent situations to produce patterns. Photography is a process which produces patterns un-limited. Set up reflections (kettle on checkerboard); multiple expose (thumbprint); use double negatives (checkered box) and photogram natural phenomenon (oil on water) – it's almost too easy!

Below: Fig. 124 The source may be natural or interfered with by man, as is our landscape and our food. It is what we make of it that counts.

probably will already have done, move on to something new. Repeats mean that records of how the work was made, and perhaps preparatory drafts, must be filed. This encourages the type of training which, however boring it may be, is one where careful notes are kept of all materials and methods. This unfortunately can be inhibiting in terms of creativity, because it tends to stop the sort of playing around necessary to produce unusual results. Having to be conscious of what one is doing, so that it may be recorded, is like adding too much hardener to the mix causing it to gel too soon.

So much sensitive and original work is tentative and searching, simply because if it were sure and confident, it would probably also be tried and tested, safe and boring.

A great number of people may be creative on their own terms but fall down when the limitations are severe. Training therefore should insist on some projects where colours or other materials are restricted in number or variety. The results of this are often misunderstood by fellow students and teachers because the results are less exciting than they could be. As you may have realized, I am a firm believer in 'much out of little'. I would give far more credit to a student who could create a design from a speck of dust than, say, to a student who had been sent to study the effect of light in Montmartre when making a study of a bottle of Coke would have taught her more. The super-realism of the mundane presented in the lithographs of Michael English has done just this, but I hope he hasn't started a cult for the super-mundane because any cult soon has its blind, slavish disciples. The importance lies in *having ideas*, not in celebrating rubbish.

It is easy to miss the point. Often a project cannot be written down in terms of a brief because you are hoping that the student will take or make a problem and move *laterally* instead of along a prescribed line. But there are occasions when 660 square inches of painted paper are exhibited. It is an obvious failure but someone says 'That's a nice piece in the corner, blow that up'. So we next look at it as a postage stamp expanded on a sheet of imperial paper. Again it is a mess and the process is repeated. This is *not* creditworthy improvization. Art and design should be attacked and defended. The *only time* work from textile students should be judged without a label or verbal explanation of intentions is if it is a finished piece offered for sale in the right shop. Even then the customer should be told the price, the fibre content and cleaning instructions. With wall-hangings and art forms, of course, this does not apply, as the object should speak for itself.

Genuine study and improvization are to be encouraged. Surrounded by the machinery of a technological institution, it is easy to assume that it has all been done before. But *you* could perhaps superimpose a laborious hand-process on to existing machinery. If the product is worthwhile, someone will invent a machine to do it. This, in turn, will not be a slick polished object; it may start off as 'meccano' or 'dexion'.

The learning process is full of negatives. It may be demoralizing to learn by continually making mistakes. Seeing negatives is slightly different. This requires an intellectual process. For example, if you go to an exhibition and see something you like, you will come home fired

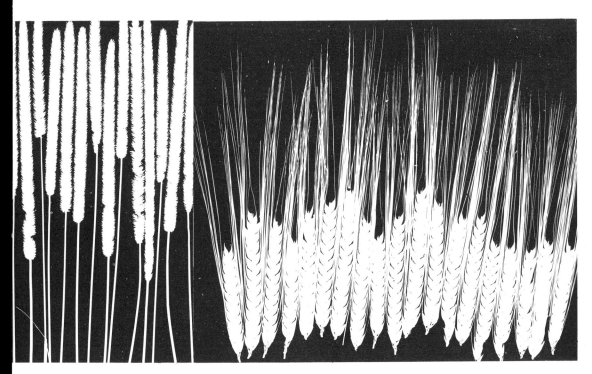

with enthusiasm. Unfortunately what you do at first may resemble or use, even subconsciously, what you have seen. If, however, you can weigh up the show in a cool way you will discover what isn't there. You could provide this later. Every time you say 'I didn't think it would be like this', consider whether you have been misled by the media which had prepared you. Consider, too, whether there is something missing that you could supply. Outsiders and beginners sometimes have great insight which they lose as they become more involved. Once involved, it is then difficult to detach yourself and see how to direct your energies. Involvement and detachment are difficult to balance.

A work which illustrates this is the stereotype once-or-twice removed project. Once removed when working from book illustrations (generally speaking this applies not to the student but to the hard-pressed designer in business), the second remove comes when you apply the first to a subject with which it has little cultural affinity. African masks typify this, and I suppose they are chosen for their dramatic qualities. The results are usually superficial in the extreme. Detachment is certainly there, but you would have to live with Africans to get sufficiently involved to use their culture to produce anything worth-while. Let's have character in our design by retaining regionalism and not by scratching at other cultures.

We have our own culture, although perhaps we need to travel to come home again and recognize it. Already we are being universalized so that our popular images are being reduced in number. The hot-dog at one end of the food chain must have pushed some subtle dishes out of existence at the other; the Volkswagen Beetle must have ousted some quainter car.

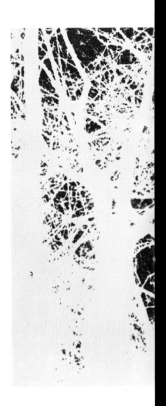

Fig. 125 Every positive must have a negative.

Studying historical ornament for design purposes is quite another approach, although partly because of sheer lack of time it would be better for a student to be told where to find his references and encouraged to study one period in depth. In this way he will gain a healthy respect for form and the reasons why it has evolved, which in turn will help him find answers to contemporary problems.

I find myself emphasizing the points which encourage a personal comment by a student. Seek out first-hand information – make your own comment. It is as well to remember that from a commercial view-point you could find yourself swimming against the tide. So you must keep up with what is happening in your own world and an eye and an ear on the wider world – especially in the popular media.

What is happening in art reflects our times and is ahead in terms of ideas. The prima-donna character artist or designer is being submerged. The abstract expressionists saw the peak of 'personal' art. Art-for-all print-making has produced some abysmal 'posters'. What will happen next?

As in textiles something visually richer will need to be produced to compete with the current fashion for antique collecting at a com-mercial level and to satisfy the psyche at a spiritual level. Art could advance through textiles as well as anything else. Some old skills should be resurrected and taught before the owners leave us for ever. The textile industry provides machinery for making bigger designs than even before. Dyeing yarns with onion skins and such like should be left to people who have not the control to use man-made dyes to produce

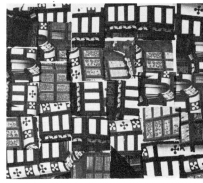

Right: Fig. 126 You may travel miles to seek inspiration (Little Moreton Hall, Cheshire) or find it in the gutter.

the subtle colours that nature makes so easily. With more resources than ever before in man's history, why don't we produce both better art and better craftsmanship? Is it that we have our priorities wrong?

The prospective patrons of aestheticism in the twentieth century are greater in number than ever before because of the distribution of wealth. But is it because we are still in the throes of the battle for fair shares that we have not yet noticed that some things are more beautiful than others? Nowadays good design is a commodity we can often afford.

FURTHER READING

Arnheim, R., *Art and Visual Perception* (London 1967).

Aslib Textile Group Members, *A Guide to Sources of Information in the Textile Industry* (London and Manchester 1970).

Bann and others, *Four Essays on Kinetic Art* (London 1966).

Brearley, A., *Worsted* (London 1964); *The Woollen Industry* (London 1965).

Carr, F., Innes, B. and Warde, B. *Screen Process Printing* (London 1961).

de Bono, E., *The Five-day Course in Thinking* (London 1968).

de Sausmarez, M., *Basic design: the dynamics of visual form* (London 1964).

Farr, M., *Design Management* (London 1966).

Glegg, G. L., *The Design of Design* (London 1969).

Gombrich, E. H., *Art and Illusion* (London 1962).

Gregory, R. L., *Eye and Brain* (London 1966).

Hickethier, A., *Colour Matching and Mixing* (London 1970).

Itten, J., *The Art of Colour* (New York 1961; London 1961).
        Design and Form; the basic course at the Bauhaus (London 1964).

Klee, Paul, *The Thinking Eye*, ed. J. Spiller, trans. R. Manheim (London 1961).

Kepes, G., *Module, Symmetry and Proportion* (London 1966).

Marsh, J. T., *An Introduction to Textile Finishing* (London 1947; reprint 1967).

Matthews, M., *Textile Fibres* (New York 1954; London 1954).

Miller, E., *Textiles: Properties and Behaviour* (London 1968).

Moncrieff, R. W., *Man Made Fibres* (London 1963).

Munsell, A. H., *A Grammar of Colour,* ed. F. Birren (New York 1969; London 1970).

Robinson, A. T. C. and Marks, R., *Woven Cloth Construction* (London 1917).

Thompson, d'Arcy, *Growth and Form* (London 1963).

Vernon, M. D., *The Psychology of Perception* (London 1965).

Watson, W., *Textile Design and Colour* (London 1954).

Weber, K. *An Introduction to the Stitch Formations in Warp Knitting* (W. Germany).

Wignall, H., *Knitting* (London 1967).

INDEX

Bold figures refer to illustrations